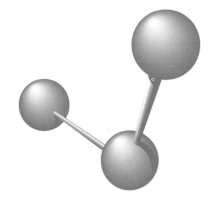

Computer Concepts and Windows®

Revised February 2003

RUSSEL STOLINS
Santa Fe Community College

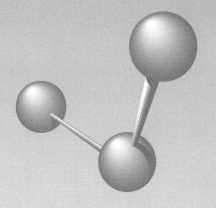

Computer Concepts and Windows®

Revised February 2003

LABYRINTH
PUBLICATIONS®

Copyright © 2003 by Labyrinth Publications

Labyrinth Publications
3314 Morningside Drive
El Sobrante, California 94803
800.522.9746
On the Web at **labpub.com**

Vice President of
Marketing and Sales: David Gauny

Editorial Director: Laura A. Lionello

Production Management,
Design and Publishing Consultation:
Seventeenth Street Studios

Composition: Seventeenth Street Studios

Printer: Courier, Kendallville

ISBN 1-59136-017-X

Manufactured in the United States of America.

10 9 8 7 6 5 4

Contents

Introduction to Labyrinth

Welcome to Labyrinth Publications, where you'll find your course to success. Our real world, project-based approach to education helps students grasp concepts—not just read about them—and prepares them for success in the workplace. Our books are written in straightforward, easy-to-follow language that is perfect for instructor-led classes and self-paced labs. At Labyrinth, we're dedicated to one purpose: delivering quality courseware that is comprehensive, effective, and affordable. It's no wonder that in just 10 years Labyrinth has become a recognized leader in Microsoft Office and operating systems courseware.

Labyrinth offers two primary courseware series for educational and professional training:

ProStart Series

Formerly our Off to Work Series, the full-length ProStart Series walks students through each application, from basics to advanced. These lessons are comprehensive and easy to read. The new ProStart Series offers many enhancements over previous versions, including streaming media videos for every lesson and a revised page design for increased clarity. New to this series is the Office XP Comprehensive Course. This book is ideal for introductory computer classes and also offers advanced topics, such as mail merge and projects with in-depth integration between applications.

Briefcase Series

A popular choice for schools and industry training programs, the Briefcase Series is designed for short-term classes and accelerated one-, two-, and three-day workshops. Each lesson is broken down into subtopics that provide quick access to key concepts. The result is a unique structure ideal for fast-paced lecturing. Briefcase books work well in 6- to 8-hour instructor-led workshops and self-paced courses lasting 25- to 35-hours. To ensure reinforcement of skills, the Briefcase Series now includes all of the end-of-lesson exercises found in the ProStart Series.

New Features for Labyrinth Courseware

Streaming Video Demonstrations

Labyrinth now offers on-screen video demonstrations to supplement key exercises. These provide another layer of instruction that is particularly beneficial to audiovisual learners. Videos are immediately available from the Labyrinth website at **labpub.com** (under Student Resources) in streaming and downloadable formats. These videos are also available to schools on CD-ROM, though not to students directly. See your Labyrinth sales representative for details.

WebSim Multimedia Content

No-cost multimedia supplements for classrooms are also available. From art and photography to entire web-based simulations that supplement the text, WebSims offer multiple benefits to both students and instructors:

- Content is always available, eliminating confusion caused by web pages that have been changed or removed.

- Simulations offer better classroom control, preventing students from wandering to unrelated sites.

- Network firewalls and restrictions on student email accounts can be circumvented, minimizing security issues while providing a full learning experience.

WebSims are immediately available from the Labyrinth website at **labpub.com** (under Student Resources). They're also available to schools on CD-ROM, though not to students directly. See your sales representative for details.

Enhanced Instructor Resources

To back your success, Labyrinth has improved the instructor support package for the ProStart and Briefcase Series texts. For example, the new instructor support CD-ROM features a graphic user-interface for easier navigation to a host of available support materials. Features include:

- Printer-friendly solutions guides, additional project-based Assessment exercises, and comprehensive course outlines and lecture notes.

- TestComposer™ software that allows convenient Microsoft Word editing. New test bank questions can now be sorted by lesson and topic, rather than by question type. Each lesson includes dozens of true/false and multiple choice questions, all of which can be modified using the TestComposer™ software.

- Complete PowerPoint presentations for every ProStart and Briefcase title to bring lectures to life.

Instructors can also visit the new Labyrinth website at **labpub.com** for additional resources, including online discussion boards for sharing ideas and the new Projects Page for downloading or posting projects created for classroom use. Look under the Educators Resource section.

Concept discussions are concise and use illustrations for added clarity.

Important information is highlighted with icons placed in the margin. Reference items and tips are presented without cluttering the page.

Quick Reference tables provide summaries of the steps needed to complete key tasks. A list of these tables appears at the beginning of the book, providing excellent at-a-glance reference.

Hands-On exercises immediately follow concept discussions to reinforce learning. As a result, students spend less time reading and more time in the applications.

Tightly integrated text and screen captures clearly demonstrate topics—perfect for instructor-led and self-paced classes.

AutoSum

The power of Excel becomes apparent when you begin using formulas and functions. The most common type of calculation is when a column or row of numbers is summed. In fact, this type of calculation is so common that Excel provides the AutoSum function specifically for this purpose.

The AutoSum Σ button on the Standard toolbar automatically sums a column or row of numbers. When you click AutoSum, Excel proposes a range of numbers. You can accept the proposed range or drag in the worksheet to select a different range. When you complete the entry, Excel inserts a SUM function in the worksheet, which adds the numbers in the range.

FROM THE KEYBOARD
ALT +⊡ for AutoSum

QR

QUICK REFERENCE: EXPLODING PIE CHARTS

Explode one slice.	■ Click once to select the entire pie.
	■ Click the slice you wish to explode.
Explode all slices.	■ Click once to select the pie.
	■ Drag any slice (without clicking first), and all slices will separate.

 Hands-On 1.9 Use AutoSum

In this exercise, you will use AutoSum to calculate several totals. Keep in mind that this section provides an introduction to formulas. You will learn more about formulas as you progress through this course.

Calculate One Column Total

1. Click Cell C8.
2. Click the AutoSum Σ button.
3. Follow these steps to review the formula and complete the entry.

	A	B	C	D
1	Computer Depot Weekly Sales Data			
2			Wednesday	Thursday
3				
4	PCs			
5		Compaq	3	10
6		IBM	4	8
7		Acer	6	13
8		Total	=SUM(C5:C7)	

Ⓐ Notice that Excel proposes the formula =SUM(C5:C7) in Cell 8 and in the Formula bar. All formulas begin with an equal (=) sign. SUM is a built-in function that adds the numbers in a range (in this example the range is C5:C7).

Ⓑ Notice the flashing marquee surrounding the range C5:C7. AutoSum assumes you want to add together all cells above C8 until the first empty cell is reached. The marquee identifies this range of cells.

Ⓒ Click the Enter ✓ button on the Formula bar to complete the entry. The total should be 13.

(Continued on the next page)

Lessons end with brief true/false and multiple choice sections, but the teaching goes much further. Project-based Skill Builder exercises present hands-on projects with only moderate assistance, while project-based Assessment exercises offer less assistance and require even more independent thought. Finally, Critical Thinking exercises provide complex word problems to thoroughly test skill mastery.

🏋 Skill Builders

Skill Builder 6.1 **Create a Column Chart**

In this exercise, you will create a column chart to display student enrollments at a university.

Expand a Series

1. Open the workbook named Skill Builder 6.1.
   Notice that the enrollment data has been completed in Column B, but the years have not been completed in Column A. Notice the first two years (1985 and 1986) form the beginning of the series 1985–2001. The best way to expand this series is with the fill handle.
2. Select Cells A4 and A5.
3. Drag the fill handle down to Row 20 to expand the series.
4. Left align 🖺 the years in Column A.

Distance Learning Courses

Labyrinth offers quality distance learning courses for WebCT and Blackboard platforms that leverage the strengths of both online and print-based content to deliver a rich learning experience. These platforms provide everything instructors need to get their classes up and running, including a customization guide so that instructors can modify courses to meet their specific curriculum requirements and teaching styles.

WebCT and Blackboard Courseware Features

Instructors and students can experience the promise of the Internet for online teaching and learning, campus communities, and integration of web-enabled student services. Labyrinth's distance learning courses run on Blackboard and WebCT Standard and Campus editions and are available for various Off to Work and ProStart titles, including the Office XP Comprehensive Course, Office XP Essentials Course, Word 2002, and Excel 2002 texts. Each lesson contains multimedia resources and online Concepts Review and Assessment tests that can be used as-is or customized to meet individual teaching styles. Production tasks for testing are also included—complete with instructions on how to deliver assignments as email attachments and with drop-box features. Another feature of Labyrinth's distance learning courses is online multimedia, including highly compressed streaming videos that are easily delivered over modem-based Internet connections.

To find out more about implementing a Blackboard or WebCT distance-learning program at your campus, please contact your Labyrinth sales representative.

Company Contact Information

To learn more about Labyrinth products and resources, or to find a sales representative in your area, please visit our website at labpub.com.

Labyrinth's dedicated customer service staff is available to assist you with ordering, billing, and any other issue between 7:30 AM and 5:00 PM [PST].

Labyrinth Publications, Inc.
3314 Morningside Dr.
El Sobrante, CA 94803
(800) 522-9746
(510) 222-7925 Fax
custserv@labpub.com

Quick Reference Index

Quick Reference tables contain generic instructions for performing tasks. They can be useful if you forget how to perform a particular task. You can use Quick Reference instructions to perform tasks long after your course is complete. The following index lists all Quick Reference procedures in *Computer Concepts and Windows*.

Visual Conventions

This book uses many visual and typographic cues to guide you through the lessons. These pages provide examples and describe the function of each cue.

Type this text   Anything you should type at the keyboard is printed in this typeface.

 Tips, Notes, and Warnings are used throughout the text to draw attention to certain topics.

Command→Command   Indicates multiple selections to be made from a menu bar. For example: File→Save means you should click the File command in the menu bar, then click the Save command on the menu.

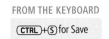 These margin notes indicate shortcut keys for executing a task described in the text. For example, (CTRL)+(S) to save your work.

 Quick Reference tables provide generic instructions on how to perform tasks. You should not perform instructions in Quick Reference tables unless you are told to do so in a Hands-On exercise.

 Multimedia videos for various topics in the text are on the labpub.com Web site. The video icons specify topics for which multimedia support is available.

 This icon indicates the availability of a Web-based simulation for a Hands-On exercise. You may need to use Web-based exercises if your computer lab is not set up to support particular exercises.

 Hands-On exercises are introduced immediately after concept discussions. They provide detailed step-by-step tutorials, allowing you to master the skills introduced in the concept discussions.

 Concepts Review questions are true/false and multiple choice questions designed to gauge your understanding of concepts.

 Skill Builder exercises provide additional hands-on practice and may introduce variations on techniques.

 Assessment exercises are designed to assess your skills. They describe the results you should achieve, without providing specific instructions.

 Critical Thinking exercises are the most challenging. They provide general instructions, allowing you to use your skills and creativity to achieve the result you envision.

Additional Learning Resources

Web Site

This book has a Web site designed to support the lessons and to provide additional learning resources. The URL for the main Web page is labpub.com/learn/bc/ccw. Some of the items you will find on the Web pages of both the ProStart and Briefcase series titles are described below.

Student Exercise Diskette Files

If the text contains an exercise diskette, then the files on the original diskette are available for download on the Web page.

Downloads

Required course files can be downloaded on the lesson pages.

Links to Multimedia Videos

Each lesson page contains links to multimedia videos. The videos can be accessed in streaming media format or downloaded to a hard drive.

Web Based Simulations

Some books in the series contain topics that have Web-based simulations. These simulations can be accessed through the lesson pages.

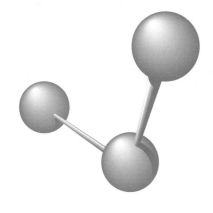

Computer Concepts and Windows®

Revised February 2003

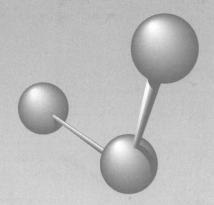

LESSON 1

Computer Concepts

When most people look inside a typical desktop computer, they see a bewildering array of cables, circuit boards, wires, and computer chips. However, the primary components of a computer system are easier to understand than you might expect. In this lesson, you will learn about the physical components of computer systems (hardware) and the logical components (software). You will learn how a computer system's hardware and software work together to help you work, play games, and access the Internet. By the end of this lesson, you should be able to identify the primary components of a typical computer system and make sense of the computer specifications featured in advertisements.

See the Lesson 1 Web Page at: labpub.com/learn/bc/ccw/lesson1

Case Study

Karen wants to purchase a computer system that will effectively meet her needs. Depending on the types of work she expects to perform on the computer, some features and capabilities will be more valuable than others. Here are some examples.

If she uses the system primarily for . . .	She will want these types of features . . .
Browsing the Internet	A basic system with a fast modem and an ink-jet printer
Desktop publishing	A fast system with a large monitor and a laser printer
Computer games	The latest video hardware for 3-D graphics
Video editing	A Firewire port that connects the computer to her digital video camera and a very large hard drive on which to edit videos

Getting the Most for Your Money

!TIP!

Spend your money on features and performance that make a tangible difference in your productivity and enjoyment.

The fastest, most feature-packed system is not necessarily Karen's best choice. She needs a balanced system, with all of its parts able to perform efficiently. For example, if she spends less money on the microprocessor (the computer's "brain"), she will have more money to spend on a better printer, a larger monitor (screen), and other features that could make the computer more useful for its primary tasks. The latest and fastest hardware almost always costs more than the previous generation, even though the previous generation may be just slightly slower.

Obsolescence

As Karen considers the purchase of a new computer system, she worries that it could soon become outdated. She even feels tempted to wait a few months for the next generation of technology to become available. Here are two factors she should keep in mind:

- Every computer eventually becomes obsolete—that is, unable to run the software you must use to get work done. But most new computers can keep up with developments for at least three to four years. That is enough time to benefit from your investment.

- If Karen waits several months for the next generation of computers, that is time she could have spent learning how to use the computer and becoming more productive. This time could be worth hundreds or even thousands of dollars to her. For example, it could lead to a better job or a promotion.

Learning the Basics

Before she makes her purchase decision, Karen decides to learn more about what's inside the computer itself. This has always been a mystery to her, but a friend explained that it's not really all that complicated to understand the basic components of the computer and the functions they perform.

Computer Systems

A computer system is a complex machine built with various mechanical parts, electronic circuits and program codes. All of these components must work together precisely. Later topics will explain many of these components in detail. This topic describes the most basic classifications of computer systems.

Basic Components

All the components of a computer system can be grouped into two types:

- **Hardware**—Hardware is the physical part of the computer system. Examples of hardware are the keyboard, the monitor, and any other physical component of the computer.

- **Software**—Software is the logical part of the computer system. Software consists of the programming instructions that let the computer interact with you to accomplish tasks. Software is typically stored on hard drives, CD-ROM disks, and floppy disks. Examples of software are Windows XP™ and Microsoft Word™.

Types of Computers

The first electronic computers were constructed in the 1940s. They were very large machines that filled a room with vacuum tubes and wiring. As computers have evolved, they have become smaller and faster. Two basic types of computers are:

- **Mainframe**—Mainframe computers can fit in a typical living room. They are designed to support large, corporate-level data processing. Hundreds of users can work simultaneously on a mainframe computer.

- **Personal Computers**—Personal computers (PCs), are small enough to fit on a desktop or inside a briefcase. A personal computer gets its computing power from a silicon chip called a microprocessor and is designed for operation by a single user.

Types of Personal Computers

There are three basic types of personal computer systems:

- **Desktop**—A desktop computer is designed to sit on top of your desk, or as a tower unit that sits alongside or under your desk. Desktop computers are easy to upgrade with new capabilities and devices.

- **Notebook**—Notebook computers are designed to be light enough to carry with you. They contain batteries, so they can operate without being plugged into a power outlet. This portability comes at a price. A notebook computer usually costs at least twice as much as a desktop computer with similar capabilities.

- **Handheld**—Handheld computers have become very popular among business users. They are very small and light and can easily fit into a purse or pocket. Also called a Personal Digital Assistant (PDA), this type of computer is designed to hook up to the user's primary computer to exchange schedules, phone numbers, and other information.

Network Servers

A network server usually looks similar to a desktop computer system, but runs special operating system software that provides network services to many other computers. Network servers let computer users share files and printers, send and receive email messages, and may also provide Internet and security services. Most personal computers used in business are connected to a network.

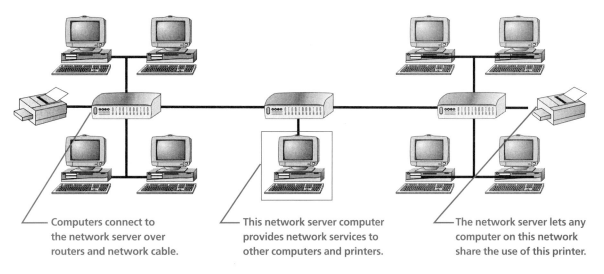

Computers connect to the network server over routers and network cable.

This network server computer provides network services to other computers and printers.

The network server lets any computer on this network share the use of this printer.

Desktop Computer Components

Desktop computer hardware is divided into the following components:

- **System Unit**—This is the box that holds the most fundamental components of the computer, such as the microprocessor, random access memory, and disk drives.

The system unit

- **Peripherals**—These are the hardware components outside the system unit. Examples of peripherals are the keyboard, mouse, monitor, and printer.

Units of Measure

The computer industry has its own terminology to describe and measure the performance and features of computer systems. These terms are explained in various sections of this lesson:

Term	What it Measures	See page ...
Bits	The most basic element of computer data	6
Bytes	The size of software files, the capacity of disk drives, and random access memory (RAM)	6
Gigahertz (GHz) Megahertz (MHz)	The speed of the computer's microprocessor	8
Resolution	The sharpness of output from a printer or the dots displayed on the computer screen	15

Bits and Bytes

The most basic unit of information on the computer is the bit. A bit is a single circuit in the computer system that is switched on or off. By itself, a bit doesn't hold much information. But if eight bits are strung together in a specific order, they form a byte. This is like interpreting the dots and dashes of Morse Code. In the examples below, notice how varying the position of a single bit changes the meaning of each byte.

Letter	Morse Code	Byte (ASCII)*
A	· —	10000001
B	— · · ·	10000010
C	— · — ·	10000011

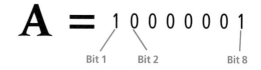

$$A = 1\ 0\ 0\ 0\ 0\ 0\ 0\ 1$$

Bit 1   Bit 2   Bit 8

*ASCII (pronounced "ask-ee") is an internationally accepted code for representing characters in the computer. It defines byte codes for 128 different alphabetic, numeric, and symbol characters. (The name is an acronym for American Standard Code for Information Interchange.)

Kilobytes and Megabytes

The table below lists the most common terms used to describe the size of software files and the capacity of random access memory, hard drives, and other storage devices explained later in this lesson.

Term	Description	Examples
Bit	A single on-off switch in a computer circuit	0 or 1
Byte	A single character of data	A, B, C, $, @, {, \
Kilobyte (KB)	Approximately one thousand bytes of data	About one single-spaced typed page of text
Megabyte (MB)	Approximately one million bytes of data	About 3 average-length novels
Gigabyte (GB)	Approximately one billion bytes of data	3,000 novels' worth of text, or about 1,500 large color pictures

NOTE! *The exact size of a kilobyte is actually 1,024 bytes. However, most people just round off those extra 24 bytes. Similarly, most people round off the extra bytes when referring to a megabyte or gigabyte.*

Inside the System Unit, Part 1

Most of a computer's processing power is determined by the components inside the system unit. Nearly all system units have an open-architecture design with modular parts that can be snapped in and out of the system. Open architecture permits the upgrading of a computer with new features and capabilities long after it is originally built. Part 1 describes the basic processing components of the system unit:

- System board
- Microprocessor
- Random access memory (RAM)
- Disk drives

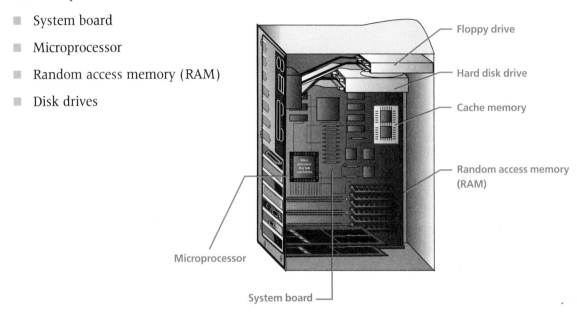

The System Board

The system board (also called the "motherboard") contains sockets and connectors that hold the essential circuitry of the computer. System boards on newer computers may also contain additional features such as built-in sound hardware and connectors to plug in disk drives.

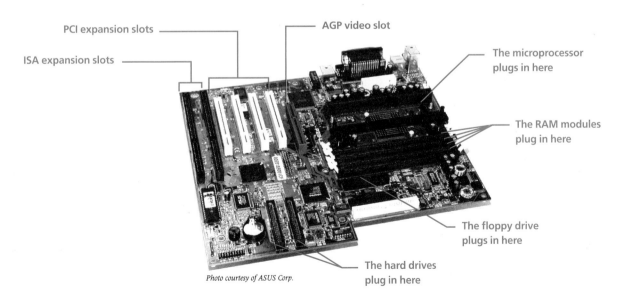

Photo courtesy of ASUS Corp.

NOTE!

See the Lesson 1 Web page for links to more information on microprocessors.

The Microprocessor

A microprocessor is a single silicon chip containing the complete circuitry of a computer. The microprocessor serves as the "brain" of a microcomputer. Because it determines the basic processing power of the computer, most advertisements start by telling you the make and model of the microprocessor. Intel's Celeron™ and Pentium 4™ series are popular microprocessors for personal computers. Advanced Micro Devices (AMD) sells a speedy competitor to Intel's Pentium 4 microprocessor called Athlon. Many used computers have Pentium II microprocessors, which run more slowly but can still perform useful work such as word processing, Web browsing, and electronic mail.

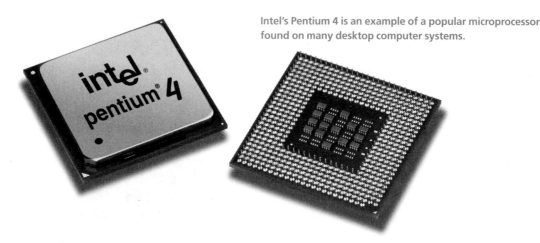

Intel's Pentium 4 is an example of a popular microprocessor found on many desktop computer systems.

Microprocessor Performance

Several design elements combine to set the performance of a microprocessor. The internal architecture of the microprocessor, its physical dimensions (die size), and the efficiency of its most basic commands (instruction set) are examples of these design elements. The quality of other components in the computer are also critical to the performance of its microprocessor. For example, a fast microprocessor in a computer equipped with very little random access memory (or RAM, described in the next major topic) may run programs more slowly than a slower microprocessor working with plenty of RAM. The most tangible factor in a microprocessor's performance is its clock speed.

Clock Speed

A microprocessor contains an internal clock that is set to a specific speed. One cycle (or one "tick" of the internal clock) is a single pulse of electrical current flowing through the microprocessor. The microprocessor carries out one action for each cycle—even if it's just registering something typed at the keyboard. Until recently the raw speed of most microprocessors was measured in megahertz (MHz), or millions of cycles per second, and most ran at almost 5MHz. The speed of the newest microprocessors is expressed in gigahertz (GHz), billions of cycles per second. Most ads for microcomputers indicate the microprocessor model and clock speed. For example: Intel Celeron/1.2 GHz, AMD Athlon/1.8 GHz, and Intel Pentium 4/2.2 GHz.

Today's most powerful microprocessors can run at speeds of 2.4 GHz or faster. This top speed rating continues to increase every few months as vendors compete to put the fastest microprocessor on the market. However, sheer speed doesn't always translate literally into performance. That's where benchmarks can be helpful.

NOTE!

See the Lesson 1 Web page for links to more information on microprocessors.

Benchmarks

How can you compare one microprocessor with another? The best method is to research their ratings on a benchmark. Benchmarks are programs that measure the performance of a computer system. You can get a good idea of the relative performance of three microprocessors when you compare their benchmark test results on similarly configured systems.

Microsoft Office Performance Benchmark

Pentium 4 2.5	174
AMD Athlon XP 1.8	165
Pentium 4 1.4	120

Benchmark tests allow you to compare the performance of microprocessors.

Cost

If you want the fastest microprocessor available, you will pay a high premium for it. The very fastest model of a microprocessor can cost up to 50% more than the models just one or two levels below it. Thus, you could pay several hundred dollars more for a microprocessor that might give you just 10% more processing speed—a speed difference you might not even be able to notice as you work with your programs. If you are purchasing your first computer and expect to run basic programs, such as a word processor or a Web browser, you are probably better off buying a microprocessor that is a few notches below the top of the line but still meets your needs. The money you save (perhaps $400 or more) could be spent on other parts of the computer, such as a larger monitor or a better printer.

Random Access Memory

Random access memory (RAM) is a special type of chip that temporarily stores data as it is processed. While the microprocessor is the single most important component inside the system unit box, RAM plays a critical role in the computer's operation. Everything you see on the computer screen is actually temporarily stored in your computer's RAM. Think of RAM as the workbench of your computer.

How RAM Works

The microprocessor never accesses software directly from the computer's disk drives. Instead, the operating system software loads software from the disk drives into RAM. Then the microprocessor reads the software from RAM for processing and places the results of processing back into RAM. The process of transferring data in and out of the microprocessor to RAM is repeated millions of times each second. The diagram below displays the sequence that one operating system, Windows, follows to run programs and process data as you work.

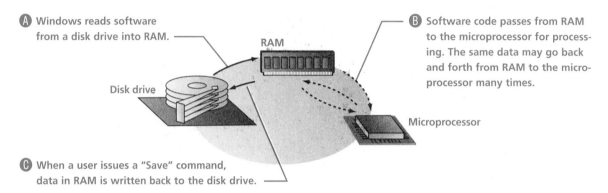

Ⓐ Windows reads software from a disk drive into RAM.

RAM

Ⓑ Software code passes from RAM to the microprocessor for processing. The same data may go back and forth from RAM to the microprocessor many times.

Disk drive

Microprocessor

Ⓒ When a user issues a "Save" command, data in RAM is written back to the disk drive.

RAM is Volatile Memory

The moment you switch off power to your computer, all of the data residing in RAM is erased. Because it can change so instantly, RAM is sometimes referred to as volatile memory. In order to safely store your work for future work sessions, you must save it to a disk drive. Since RAM temporarily stores correspondence and other work you perform on the computer, it is very important to remember to save your work before you switch off your computer.

Locations of RAM

A computer system actually has various types of RAM in several locations inside the system unit. However, when you see an advertisement describing the amount of RAM within a computer, the designation always refers to the main system RAM. Other types of RAM include cache RAM (see page 11) and video RAM (described on page 15).

Types of RAM Modules

RAM chips are on small modules that plug into special slots in the system board. The capacity of these modules is rated in megabytes (MB). Popular sizes are 128, 256, and 512 MB. There are two basic types of RAM modules found in most new computers:

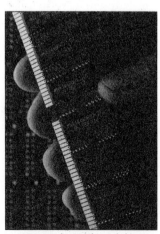

- **DDRAM**—double data rate (DDR) RAM has the potential to operate twice as fast as the older SDRAM modules. They do this by reading and writing data simultaneously (thus doubling the speed). However, to harness this potential performance boost, the design of key components of the computer system, particularly the system board and microprocessor, must be compatible with this new technology.

An SDRAM (DIMM) module

- **SDRAM**—Until recently, SDRAM modules were the most common form of RAM on new computers. These snap-in modules are reliable and easy to upgrade and replace.

Cache RAM

Most computers also come with another form of RAM called a cache (pronounced "cash"). This is expensive, high-speed RAM that stores the most recently used program code and data. Any time the microprocessor needs fresh data to process, it checks to see if any of the data it needs is already in the cache. The microprocessor can work with data in the cache much more quickly than if it must go to normal RAM or the hard drive to process the data. Modern microprocessors have internal (also called Level 1) cache memory built right into them, and external (Level 2) cache memory installed on the system board.

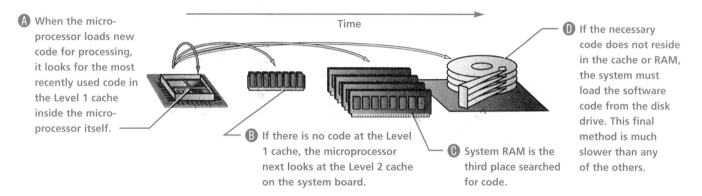

A When the microprocessor loads new code for processing, it looks for the most recently used code in the Level 1 cache inside the microprocessor itself.

Time

B If there is no code at the Level 1 cache, the microprocessor next looks at the Level 2 cache on the system board.

C System RAM is the third place searched for code.

D If the necessary code does not reside in the cache or RAM, the system must load the software code from the disk drive. This final method is much slower than any of the others.

How Much RAM Do You Need?

The system RAM in your computer is measured in megabytes. Most new computers are equipped with 256 to 512 megabytes of RAM. This is enough to run most popular programs. It is relatively easy to install additional RAM into a computer. The following points can help you determine the amount of system RAM you need for your computer:

- The more RAM your computer has, the more programs you can run simultaneously.

- Sophisticated application programs for computer graphics and databases require plenty of RAM to run efficiently. See the table on page 32 for a comparison of the RAM requirements of different types of application programs.

- When you purchase application software, the amount of system RAM necessary to run the software is indicated on the package.

Disk Drives

When software is installed on a computer, it is stored on various disk drives in the system unit. Some types of disks are fixed inside the computer, while others are removable. The various disk drives are often referred to as the computer's mass-storage devices.

Listed below are the most popular types of disk drives for personal computers. Each type has capabilities that make it ideal for particular tasks.

Drive Name	Description	Typical Capacity*
Hard Drive	A fixed (nonremovable) disk drive inside the system unit. Hard drives are very fast and can hold very large amounts of software, such as application programs and your user data files. When you install a new application program on the computer, it is stored on the hard drive.	6GB to 100GB
Floppy Drive	A floppy drive reads data from and writes data to floppy disks (also called "floppies"). Floppy disks get their name from the flexible disk within the plastic disk housing. This disk has a magnetic oxide coating similar to cassette tapes. Floppy drives are very slow compared to other types of drives, especially hard drives. Floppy disks are most convenient for carrying work to another computer.	1.4MB
CD-ROM Drive	A CD-ROM (compact disk-read only memory) drive can hold large amounts of data. CD-ROM disks look similar to music CDs but store information differently—though most CD-ROM drives can play music CDs. CD-ROM drives are rated according to transfer speed. A 40x CD-ROM drive transfers data 40 times faster than the first CD-ROM drives that appeared in the late 1980s.	650MB
CD-RW Drive	CD-RW (compact disk-read write) drives allow you to write data to blank CDs and can read data from standard CD-ROM discs. Recordable CD-ROM discs are excellent media for long-term storage of important computer files. For example, you would want to store an electronic family photo album on a recordable CD-ROM disc.	650MB
DVD Drive	A DVD (digital video disk) drive can read both DVD and CD-ROM discs. This makes it a popular compliment to a CD-RW drive on many new computers. Bundled software allows you to view DVD movies on your computer monitor.	Up to 17GB
Removable Disk Drive	A removable-disk drive stores data on disk cartridges. By adding more disk drives, you can create virtually unlimited data storage space. The Iomega Zip™ is one popular example of a removable disk drive. You can store the equivalent of about 180 floppy disks on a single Zip disk.	100MB to 250MB

*The abbreviations for capacity are KB for kilobyte, MB for megabyte, and GB for gigabyte. For a description of these, see the glossary.

How Disk Drives Work

Most hard drives use disks covered with a magnetic oxide material similar to that used for cassette tapes. A read/write head hovers over the disks as they spin at high speed (4800 to 9600 rpm). The read/write head applies positive and negative charges to the surface of the disk to record data. Each positive or negative charge represents one bit of data.

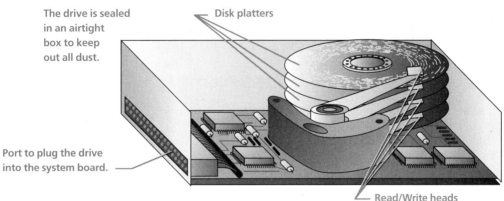

The drive is sealed in an airtight box to keep out all dust.

Disk platters

Port to plug the drive into the system board.

Read/Write heads

Primary components of a standard hard disk drive.

TIP!

Never move a computer while it is running. When the read/write heads are not in the "parked" position, there is a higher risk that they could touch the hard drive platters if the computer is moved.

Hard drives are extremely reliable, but they can be damaged. Hard drives are sealed in an air-tight box to keep out dust particles. If one of the read/write heads touches a disk, it can damage the hard drive and result in the loss of data—perhaps all of the data on the hard drive. When you switch off the computer, the read/write heads are automatically moved to a safe, "park" position, which keeps them away from the data on the hard drive.

RAM Compared to Disk Drives

Although RAM and the capacity of disk drives are both measured in megabytes, the two are very different. Many people who are new to computers confuse RAM with storage space on the disk drives. You can avoid this confusion if you think of RAM as the computer's temporary workbench memory and disk drives as the computer's permanent mass-storage devices.*

There are two important distinctions between RAM and mass storage:

- When you switch off the power to your computer, any data in RAM is erased, whereas data stored on disk drives is saved for future work sessions.

- Hard drives have far more capacity than RAM. A new computer usually has 40 or more times more hard drive storage space than the size of its RAM.

---

*The word permanent should not be taken literally. Like any electromechanical device, a disk drive might someday fail. It is also possible to inadvertently give a command to erase some or all of the data on the disk drive.

Inside the System Unit, Part 2

Although the microprocessor, RAM, and disk drives are critical to the performance of a computer, they require the support of many other components. Part 2 describes the video system that creates the image on the computer display and the expansion cards that give the computer additional capabilities.

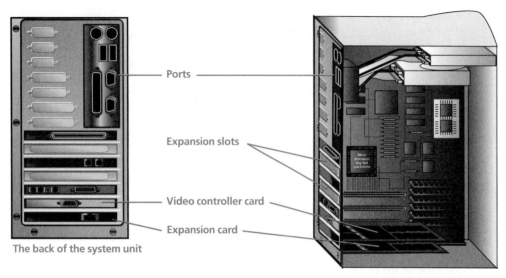

Ports

Expansion slots

Video controller card

Expansion card

The back of the system unit

Cutaway view of the system unit

Computer Video

A computer screen display is made up of hundreds of thousands of individual dots of light called pixels. Each pixel receives commands 60 to 80 times per second that control exactly which color it should display. These commands generate patterns of pixels to create the text, windows, controls, and other images you see on the screen.

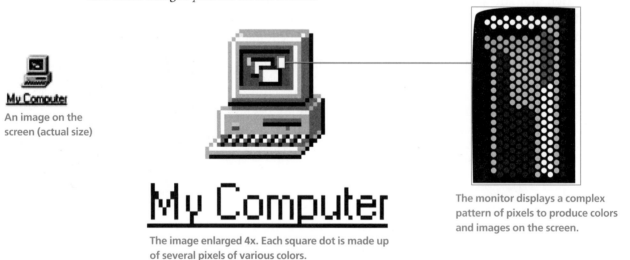

An image on the screen (actual size)

The image enlarged 4x. Each square dot is made up of several pixels of various colors.

The monitor displays a complex pattern of pixels to produce colors and images on the screen.

Key Components

Three key hardware and software components make up the video subsystem of a computer:

- **Video monitor**—Most monitors appear similar to television sets, but contain more sophisticated and precise circuitry. Video monitors come in two primary types: traditional cathode ray tube (CRT) monitors and liquid crystal display (LCD) panels.

- **Video controller**—This is an expansion card inside the computer's system unit that sends video signals to the monitor. It controls the display of all the images you see on the monitor.

- **Video driver**—This is software that tells Windows how to work effectively with the video controller card and monitor.

Video Performance

There are three important ways to measure the performance of a video controller and monitor:

- *Resolution* is the number of pixels that the monitor can display. Displaying more pixels on your monitor will make the images on your computer screen appear sharper and smaller. The most basic resolution setting is 640 pixels across by 480 pixels down (written 640 × 480). Many computers are capable of almost double this resolution at 1024 × 768.

640 × 480

800 × 600

1024 × 768

The higher your monitor's resolution setting, the smaller and sharper images will appear. The examples above show how the My Computer icon and label would appear at different resolution settings.

- The *color depth* indicates how many different colors the screen can potentially display. A higher color-depth setting gives the most accurate display of graphics. If you want to display photo-realistic color images, make sure the video controller is capable of 24-bit color, which allows the monitor to display up to 16.7 million colors. Other popular settings are 256 color (8-bit) and 64,000 color (16-bit).

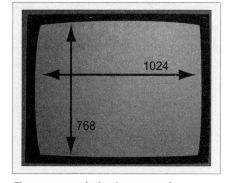

The screen resolution is measured horizontally and vertically in pixels.

- The *refresh rate* determines how fast the video controller redraws the display on the monitor. This is measured in hertz (cycles per second). A refresh rate of 70 hertz (Hz) or more gives the monitor display a very stable image, without any noticeable flicker. A refresh rate of less than 65Hz can result in noticeable flicker, which may tire your eyes during long work sessions.

Video RAM

The video controller has its own RAM that is separate from the RAM on the system board. This RAM is devoted to video display. Most computers sold today have plenty of video RAM to display millions of colors at all of the many resolutions your video controller and monitor can display.

VGA and SVGA

As you shop for a computer and monitor, you will see several popular terms used to describe video performance. Chief among the alphabet soup of acronyms will be VGA and Super-VGA. Both terms refer to a level of video performance. VGA is short for Video Graphics Array.

Term	Level of Performance
VGA	Resolution of 640 × 480 pixels, and the simultaneous display of 16 colors.
Super-VGA SVGA	Resolution of 800 × 600 pixels (or more) and the simultaneous display of 256 colors (or more). Nearly all new computers have SVGA displays or better.
XGA	Resolution of 1024 x 768 and the simultaneous display of thousands of colors.
UGA	Resolution of 1600 x 1200 and the simultaneous display of thousands of colors.

Purchasing an LCD Monitor

LCD monitors are becoming an increasingly popular replacement for standard CRT monitors. Most LCD monitors use a technique called thin film transfer (TFT) to produce a bright image that can change rapidly to display movies and animation with the necessary speed and fluidity. Compared to traditional CRT monitors, LCD monitors are much smaller and lighter, more expensive, and usually have less color range and quality.

The new generation of LCD monitors are light and bright.

Photo courtesy of iiayma, North America.

Key LCD Specifications

While many specifications and features define the quality of an LCD panel, the most important specifications are the panel's contrast ratio, viewing angle, and brightness. Other specifications indicate panel performance as well. In the final analysis, it is best to purchase an LCD monitor after you've had a chance to view it and compare it to similar monitors.

Specification	Description
Contrast ratio	This specification measures the difference between the brightest and darkest pixels (points of light) the screen can generate to form an image. The higher the contrast ratio, the greater the range of colors a panel can display.
Viewing angle	This specification measures the angle up to which you can see a clear, bright image on the screen. Images viewed on an LCD panel from outside its viewing angle will appear faded and washed out.

Purchasing a CRT Monitor

You should consider several features when purchasing a monitor. Remember that the screen resolution and refresh rate settings your monitor is capable of should also be compatible with the capabilities of your computer's video controller.

Feature	Description
Screen size	Like television screens, the size of a computer screen is measured diagonally. Most entry-level computer systems are sold with a 15" monitor. Monitors also have a viewable area rating that measures the largest screen area you can display. For example, many 17" monitors have a viewable area of 15.9 inches. A larger screen allows you to view your work comfortably at high resolution settings. This is an advantage for graphics-intensive work such as desktop publishing.
Maximum resolution	Monitors and video controllers are rated for the maximum resolution they can handle. If you set the resolution higher than the monitor is rated, the display may go blank. A high-quality monitor can display a maximum resolution of 1024 × 768 pixels or greater. Some large monitors can handle a display of 1600 × 1200 pixels. This high resolution allows the display of much more information on the screen than the standard 800 x 600 setting.
Dot pitch	Dot pitch refers to the size of the individual points of light (pixels) on the screen. A larger dot pitch causes images on the screen to appear fuzzier and coarser. High-quality monitors have a dot pitch of around .24 (written ".24 dp"). Cheaper monitors sold with bargain systems may have a dot pitch of .39 or more. *Tip: Purchase a monitor with a dot pitch of .28 or less for the best quality display.*
Vertical frequency	A vertical frequency setting of 70 hertz or better results in a very steady image with no noticeable flicker. Monitors and video controllers are rated for the maximum vertical frequency setting at which they can operate.

3-D Video Controllers

Some video controllers are specially optimized for computer games. Many of the latest computer games have some dazzling 3-D special effects. However, these special effects can appear jagged and jerky on older hardware. The latest generation of 3-D video controllers plug into system boards equipped with an Accelerated Graphics Port (AGP) and can display textured 3-D images with great speed and detail.

Expansion Cards

Expansion cards are modular circuit boards that plug into the computer to add new features and capabilities, some of which might not even have existed when the computer was manufactured. For example, you could add an expansion card to connect a scanner or video camera to the computer.

Examples of Expansion Cards

There are numerous expansion cards you can purchase and plug into your computer. Any time you buy an expansion card, it also comes with the software necessary to use its features.

Card type	Description
Modem	A modem lets you dial over a standard phone line to connect to other computers. An internal modem is installed on an expansion card. An external modem is a peripheral. (See page 22 for details on modems).
Sound	A sound card can generate high-quality sound and music on the computer. This is useful for games and programs such as online encyclopedias. Some sound cards connect to a musical keyboard so you can create your own compositions.
Video capture	The video capture card has a connector for a video camera and software that helps you capture (record) video onto your computer's hard drive. You can edit captured video to add special effects and titles. After editing, you can record the video from the hard drive back to videotape.
Network or LAN	The network card lets you connect your computer to a local area network (LAN). If you have network cards on two or more computers in your home, you can set up a small version of a LAN called a peer-to-peer network.
TV	A TV card can display a television picture in a window on your monitor. It can connect to an antenna or cable TV service. The card comes with software to tune in channels.

Expansion Slots

Expansion cards plug into expansion slots on the system board. Most computers sold today come with two types of expansion slots. Before you purchase an expansion card, you should always check to see which types of expansion slots are still open (unused). The open expansion slot and the expansion card must be of the same type.

Slot Type	Description
PCI	This is a very fast connection to your computer's microprocessor. Many new types of expansion cards are designed for this type of slot. For example, video capture and network cards are now typically designed to fit into a PCI slot. PCI is short for Peripheral Component Interconnect.
ISA	This is an older type of slot. It is not as fast as PCI, but there are still many types of expansion cards for which this slot is fast enough for good performance. ISA is short for Industry Standard Architecture.

The Bus

Expansion slots connect to the microprocessor by a data path called the bus. The speed and size of this data path have an important effect on your computer's performance. For example, PCI slots have a wide, 64-bit data path on the system bus (which sends data 64 bits at a time), while the older ISA slot data path is a narrow 16 bits. So, a PCI expansion card can exchange data with the rest of the computer system much faster than an ISA card.

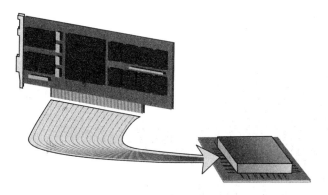

The data bus is like a highway to the system's microprocessor.

Ports

A port is a place to plug a cable or peripheral device into your computer's system unit. The keyboard, mouse, and monitor plug into ports. Many expansion cards provide additional ports for specific devices. For example, a scanner may connect to the computer through a port on an expansion card. All computer systems come with several different ports built into the back of the system unit. Various cables are designed to work with the ports. For example, you would use a parallel cable to connect a printer to the parallel port.

The table below lists the most common types of ports, and they are shown in the figure at the bottom of this page. A computer system may have some or all of these ports.

	This port type . . .	is commonly used to connect . . .
A	PS/2	a mouse and keyboard.
B	USB port	a growing variety of peripheral devices, including scanners, keyboards, cameras, and monitors.
C	Serial (Com1, Com2)	an external modem.
D	Parallel (LPT1)	a printer.
E	SCSI	a scanner or external disk drive.
F	FireWire (IEEE 1394)	a digital video camera or external hard drive.
G	Video	the monitor.
H	Miniplugs	speakers, microphone, and sound sources.
I	Joystick	a joystick for games.
J	Phone jack	a telephone line to an internal modem.
K	RS-14	a network cable.

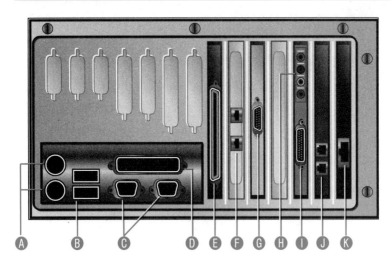

Selecting Peripherals

A peripheral is hardware outside the computer's system unit box. Peripherals are usually associated with entering data into the computer (input) or outputting data in the form of screen displays, printouts, and sound. The monitor is one example of a peripheral covered earlier in this lesson.

Plug and Play

Plug and Play devices are designed for Windows to recognize automatically. When Windows detects a new Plug and Play device, it searches for and loads the necessary software to work with the device or prompts you to perform an installation from a CD that came with the device.

USB Ports

USB (Universal Serial Bus) ports allow you to connect many different types of devices to the computer. This connection has become very popular for connecting scanners, printers, digital cameras, keyboards, mice, and other peripherals. USB ports allow you to chain several different devices to a single port on your computer. You can also plug and unplug a USB device while the computer is running. This capability is called "hot swapping." Many new computers now have two USB ports at the back of the computer (see figure on the previous page) as well as two USB ports at the front.

Keyboard

The keyboard is the main data entry device for a microcomputer. There are numerous makes of keyboards, and they can differ considerably in quality. You may want to consider an ergonomic keyboard. These spread out the keys or even split the keyboard in half to give your hands a more natural typing angle. The style and placement of the computer keyboard is an important factor in healthy computing habits. See page 33 for tips on setting up your computer with the keyboard at the proper height.

Many ergonomic keyboards have a built-in wrist rest and a curved shape for comfortable hand positioning.

The Mouse

The mouse is a pointing device to give commands to the computer by pointing and clicking at specific places on the screen. An ergonomically designed mouse fits very comfortably in your hand; some also have a third button or scroll wheel you can program to issue special commands. A typical mouse uses a small rolling ball at the bottom of the device to sense movement. An optical mouse uses a light sensor to track movement.

This cordless mouse features a scroll wheel to make browsing in data windows easier.

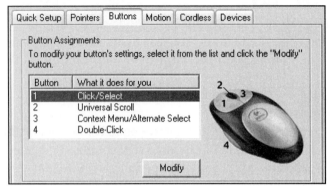

You can program certain mouse buttons and the scroll wheel to perform custom functions

Trackballs

A popular alternative to the mouse is called a trackball. It uses a rotating ball that you roll with your thumb or fingers. Some users prefer a trackball because it saves desktop space. Others find rolling the trackball more comfortable than moving a mouse. A combined trackball and mouse is also available.

Photo courtesy of Logitech

A trackball mouse can save space on your desk

Telephone Modems

A modem (MOdulator/DEModulator) is a device that translates the digital data of computer communication into analog sound waves that can be transmitted over a voice telephone line. At the other end of the line, another modem converts the sound back into digital data. With a modem you can:

■ dial up and exchange information with other computers.

■ connect to an Internet service provider (ISP) for Web browsing and email.

■ use your computer to send and receive faxes.

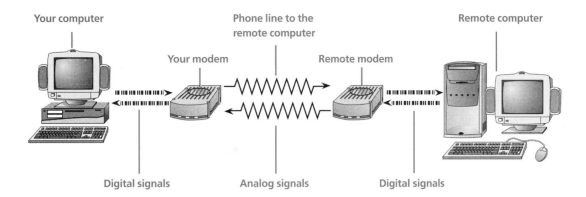

Your computer | Phone line to the remote computer | Remote computer

Your modem | Remote modem

Digital signals | Analog signals | Digital signals

Types of Telephone Modems

Modems come in both external and internal models. Internal modems are expansion cards you can plug into an expansion slot inside the system unit. An external modem is a peripheral that sits on your desk and plugs into the back of your computer with a serial cable. Most new computers come with an internal modem as standard equipment. Some modems even offer voice mail capabilities (for example: "To leave a message for Bob, dial 1; to leave a message for Sue, dial 2," and so on).

Photo courtesy of 3Com Corporation.

Modem Speed

A faster modem is useful if you frequently browse the Web. You measure a modem's speed as the bits per second of digital data it can transmit over a telephone line under ideal conditions. For example, under ideal conditions a 56K modem can send and receive data at nearly 56,000 bits per second (or about 7,000 bytes per second). However, telephone line quality, the facilities of Internet service providers, and other factors may reduce a modem's actual speed to less than its rated speed.

Other Types of Modems

Most modems in use today work on standard telephone lines. However, a new generation of telecommunications technology is beginning to replace phone modems. These technologies are becoming widely available in major metropolitan areas.

- A *cable modem* allows you to access the Internet at speeds up to 35 times faster than standard phone modems. Cable modems connect to the same cables that carry cable television signals.

- *DSL* (Digital Subscriber Line) modems offer data speeds up to 50 times faster than a telephone modem. DSL modems connect to a standard telephone line.

Scanners

A scanner turns pictures and photographs into computer files that you can place into documents or attach to email messages. Flatbed scanners work similarly to copy machines. You place the original face down the scanner's glass plate, then run software to select and scan the part of an image you wish to save as a computer file.

Photo courtesy of Hewlett-Packard Corp.

Scanning Software

Every scanner comes with bundled software to install on the computer. This software allows you to scan and edit pictures and photographs. Additional bundled software may allow you to use the scanner as a copier or fax machine (in conjunction with a modem). Some scanners even come with optical character recognition (OCR) software that converts printed pages from books, magazines, and newspapers into text you can edit in a word processor.

You use the bundled software to control the scanner.

Printers

A printer is a very useful peripheral for many types of work. A printer can help you create professional looking documents, custom business cards, large signs, and other types of printouts. Modern printers produce very sharp output inexpensively and quickly. Two types of printers work best for home and office use:

- **Laser**—Laser printers use a laser to trace a pattern on a drum that picks up toner and fuses it to the paper to print text and graphics. Laser printers are very fast and they print sharp images; however, most laser printers print only in black and white. Color laser printers cost more than black-and-white models. A good color laser printer costs about twice as much as an equivalent black and white model.

- **Ink-jet**—These printers spray microscopic drops of ink on the page. Compared to laser printers, ink-jets are slower and cannot print as sharply. But most ink-jet printers are capable of color printing. When used with special paper, and set to a low speed, some ink-jet printers can create photo-realistic color pictures.

There are two important measures of printer performance:

- The resolution of printing is measured in dots per inch (DPI). The higher the resolution of a printout, the sharper the appearance of graphics and text on the page. Early laser printers and most ink-jet printers can print up to 600 DPI. Most new laser printers now print at 1200 DPI.

- The speed of a printer is typically measured as the number of pages per minute (PPM) it is able to print.

The table below is a generalized comparison of laser and ink-jet printers.

Printer Type	Speed	Prints color	Printer resolution printing in . . .	
			Color	Black and White
Laser	6–24 PPM	No	N/A	600–1200 DPI
Color Laser	6 PPM color 18 PPM b/w	Yes	600 DPI	1200 DPI
Ink-Jet	2–5 PPM color 5–9 PPM b/w	Yes	300 DPI	600 DPI

Digital Camera

Digital cameras have become a popular way of taking photographs that are easy to transfer over the Internet and copy to a CD-ROM disc. The number of pixels it can capture in a single shot measures the capability of most cameras. For example, a 1-mega pixel camera can take a picture composed of approximately 1 million pixels. A 3.35-mega pixel camera can take photographs that result in a clear 8" x 10" printed image. Most digital cameras rely on a removable memory cartridge to store photos. Some digital cameras can also take small movies with sound.

The Nikon CoolPix 4500 is an example of a digital camera.

Attribution: Photo courtesy of Nikon USA.

Digital Video Camera

Digital video cameras are similar to traditional video cameras, except that they capture and store video as a series of digital images instead of as analog images on videotape. Digital video cameras can store images on various media, including memory cards, digital videotape, and CDs. One advantage of digital video cameras is that it is easy to transfer the video to a computer via a USB or FireWire (IEEE 1394) connection. Since the video is already digitized, you can use software to edit it and apply special effects.

Surge Protector

A computer has very sensitive circuitry. A power surge can burn out the most important and expensive components of your computer. To prevent this, your computer and its peripherals should always be connected to a surge protector. Most computer hardware also requires a grounded (three-prong) power outlet. Some surge protectors come with several on-off switches for the outlets. This is very convenient, since it makes switching off individual components of the computer system when they are not in use easy to do.

Photo courtesy of Kensington Technology Group.

Uninterruptible Power Source

If your electrical utility is subject to frequent blackouts and brownouts, you should consider the purchase of an uninterruptible power source (UPS). This device contains a power sensor that instantly switches to a high-capacity battery any time the power to your computer is cut off. The UPS will also sound an audible tone that warns you the computer is running off the battery. The amount of time a UPS can keep the computer running depends on the size of the UPS battery and the computer's power requirements. Typically, the UPS should be able to power the computer for at least five minutes. This provides enough time to save your work and shut down the computer normally.

An example of a UPS for home or office computer.

Photo courtesy American Power Conversion Corporation.

Computer Software

Computer software is the invisible, logical component of the computer. Most software exists in the form of program instructions that control how the computer functions and performs tasks for you. Software also stores the results of the work you perform on the computer. Without software, a computer is useless.

COMPUTER SOFTWARE		
Program Files		**User Files**
Operating Systems	**Applications**	
Windows XP	Word	Letter
Windows 98	Excel	Digital Photo
Macintosh System X	Internet Explorer	Name & address list
Linux 3.3	Quicken	Web page
DOS 6.0	Outlook Express	Digital Video clip

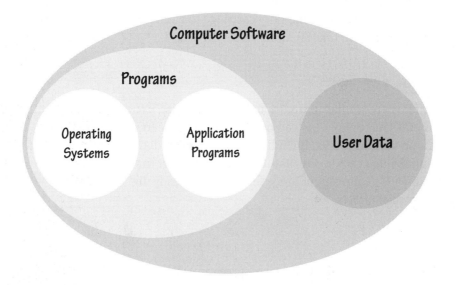

Files

The basic unit of software is the file. A file is a collection of computer data that has some common purpose. Examples of files are application programs, digital images, or a letter you have typed. Depending on the programs you install and use, the computer may have thousands of files stored on its disk drive.

Programs

A program is software code designed to run the computer and help you get work done. A simple program can be a single software file. Complex programs like Word and Excel are made up of dozens of files, each of which helps you use some feature of the program. There are two basic types of programs in a computer system: the operating system and application programs.

Operating System

The operating system (OS) is the basic software your computer needs in order to run. The operating system software takes control of the computer soon after it is turned on and controls all of the basic functions of your computer. The operating system also helps you browse through and organize your user files (see the next page). This makes finding and opening documents and other types of work you have created previously easier.

Navigate to the Web page for this lesson to view a video on checking system properties in Windows. (Viewing this video is optional.)

Every computer requires an operating system in order to function. Windows XP is an operating system. Other popular operating systems include System X for the Macintosh, Windows 98, Linux, and Unix.

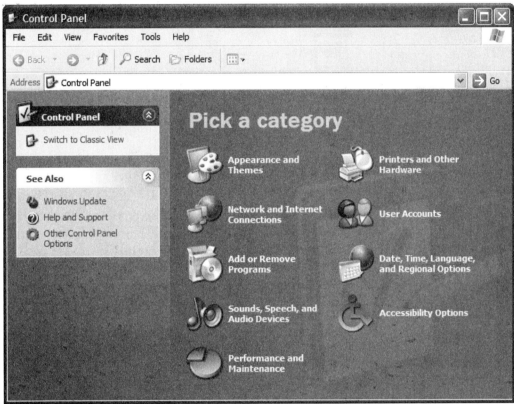

Most of the settings in the Windows XP Control Panel are controlled by the operating system.

Examples of the Operating System at Work

Here are two examples of how the operating system plays a vital role in every task you perform on the computer:

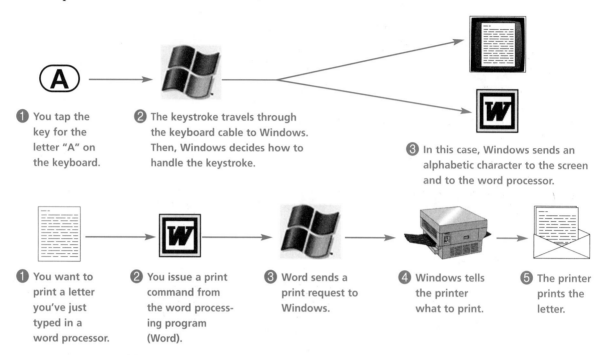

1 You tap the key for the letter "A" on the keyboard.

2 The keystroke travels through the keyboard cable to Windows. Then, Windows decides how to handle the keystroke.

3 In this case, Windows sends an alphabetic character to the screen and to the word processor.

1 You want to print a letter you've just typed in a word processor.

2 You issue a print command from the word processing program (Word).

3 Word sends a print request to Windows.

4 Windows tells the printer what to print.

5 The printer prints the letter.

Application Programs

Application programs (or simply "applications") help you accomplish tasks. For example, you use a word processing program to type letters and create other documents. You can use financial management programs to balance checkbooks and investment accounts. You use graphics programs to create drawings and other graphic art. Even games for entertainment are a form of application program. Here are some examples of popular application programs:

This application . . .	helps you to . . .
Word	write letters, memos, reports, and other text documents.
Excel	work with numbers on a spreadsheet.
Outlook	keep a schedule, and send and receive electronic mail messages.
Access	keep track of large amounts of data.
PowerPoint	create on-screen presentations.
Internet Explorer	browse sites on the World Wide Web.
Photoshop	edit and add special effects to photographs.
PageMaker	create newsletters, flyers, and books.
Quicken	write checks and keep track of your personal finances.
TurboTax	fill out tax forms and print a tax return, or file the return electronically.
FrontPage	create your own Web sites.
Windows Movie Maker	create and combine your own digital videos by adding titles and special effects.

User Files

User files (or simply "files") contain information and work that users have created in application programs. When you finish a piece of work, you will usually save it as a file on a hard drive or floppy disk. Examples of work you might store in user files are a:

- letter you typed and saved with a word processor

- drawing or digital photograph

- database of names and addresses

- record of your checking account transactions

- game you have saved to play later

Computer Viruses

A computer virus is a software program designed to cause trouble on a computer system. Viruses can invisibly transmit themselves to "infect" a computer without your knowledge. For example, if you copy a virus-infected program to a floppy disk, then run that program on another computer, the virus may infect other programs on the new "host" computer. There are many types of computer viruses, and new ones are discovered almost every day. Most viruses are harmless, but a very few have been known to do great damage, such as erase your hard drive!

Antivirus Software

A special type of application software designed to detect and erase viruses is called an antivirus program. It is a good idea to purchase and install antivirus software on a new computer. An antivirus program watches all software activities on the computer, and halts the processing of any program it considers to be performing a "suspicious" activity. Antivirus programs can detect the unseen activities of most viruses when they try to invade your system and can usually "clean" (erase) a virus in an infected file.

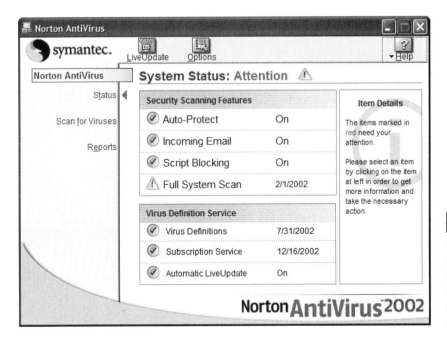

This antivirus program loads itself automatically when the computer is powered up. It watches for suspicious activity that could indicate a virus attempting to infect the system.

Macro Viruses

A new type of virus has emerged in the past few years. These are small programs embedded in word processor and spreadsheet document files. These macro viruses are the first viruses not contained inside program files. (A macro is a saved series of keystrokes and commands that you can "replay" to perform repetitive tasks.) Most modern antivirus software can detect and clean macro viruses.

Virus Definition Updates

New strains (types) of computer virus are discovered almost daily. Since many viruses use similar techniques to invisibly "infect" a computer system, many antivirus programs can detect new strains of virus without having detailed information about them. If the computer has a connection to the Internet or is equipped with a modem, many antivirus programs can utilize a special updating feature. This feature dials out and copies (downloads) the most up-to-date virus definitions onto your hard drive. These updates can ensure that your antivirus program has the latest information on new types of viruses.

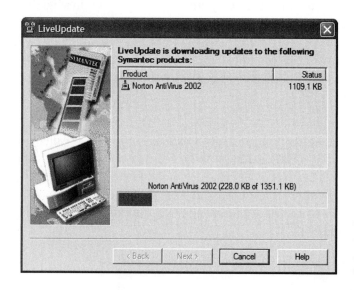

This screen walks a user through contacting the vendor for the latest virus definitions. Most antivirus software vendors offer a free one-year subscription to this type of update service.

Researching Software

Before you shop for hardware, you should always begin by researching the software you expect to run. Why? Because the usefulness of your new computer depends on its ability to run the application programs that help you complete tasks, and to store the data files you create as you work. Some application programs require a more powerful computer than others.

Examples

You want to send and receive electronic mail (email) over the Internet. Email application programs are generally pretty simple, and even a very inexpensive computer can run them. However, what if you also want to run the latest generation of voice dictation software? These programs allow you to speak into a microphone, with the computer "typing" every word you say. Then you can revise your dictation in a word processor. This type of software makes very high demands on the computer's hardware. If the computer's hardware does not meet the program's requirements, it will not be able to run the voice dictation program at all.

Reading Software Requirements

When you purchase software in a store, the package will indicate the type of hardware and operating system required to run the software. Before you purchase a computer, you should examine the packaging of programs you intend to run. Pay close attention to all of the requirements specified for each program. This research will help you determine exactly which features and equipment are necessary and most valuable. For example, you may discover that the fastest microprocessor on the market will not be as useful to you as more RAM.

Making Your Purchase Decision

Once you have completed your software research, you are ready to make your purchase decision. The table below summarizes the basic specifications to keep in mind when you shop for your computer.

Requirement	Notes	Examples
Microprocessor	This specification tells you the model and speed of the microprocessor required to run the software. A slower or older model microprocessor may not be able to handle the demands of a sophisticated application program. On the other hand, many basic programs will run fine with the slower microprocessor you might find in a used computer.	Pentium 4, 3.2 GHz Celeron, 1.8 GHz Athlon, 2.2 GHz
Operating system	Application programs are designed to run with specific versions of Windows or some other operating system. Most programs designed for earlier versions of Windows will also (but not always) work smoothly with a later version of Windows.	Windows 98 or later Windows 2000 Professional Windows XP Home Edition Macintosh System X
RAM	More sophisticated programs typically require more RAM to run efficiently. If you intend to run several programs at once, you probably want to have at least twice as much RAM as is required by the most demanding program you will run.	64 MB of RAM with Windows 98 or ME 96 MB of RAM with Windows XP
Hard drive storage space	Some programs require a large amount of space on your hard drive to run efficiently. There may be a minimal installation option that takes less hard drive space, and a full installation option that installs all the optional features of the program.	60 to 110 GB on the hard drive
CD-ROM or DVD drive	You will install most programs from a CD-ROM disc. Computer DVD drives can also read CD-ROM discs. Some very large programs (such as encyclopedias) may be available on DVD disc.	32x CD-ROM drive DVD drive
Extras	Some software applications may recommend additional hardware to provide more value from the program.	56K modem Cable modem Firewire (IEEE 1394) port

Recommended versus Minimum Configurations

Many software programs list both minimum and recommended hardware configurations. Below is a practical comparison between these two types of requirements, followed by three examples.

- **Minimum**—This configuration is satisfactory only if you intend to run programs on your computer only occasionally and only for brief periods of time. Running the program in the minimum configuration may cause your computer to operate very slowly. This can be frustrating if you are trying to work efficiently to meet a deadline.

- **Recommended**—This hardware configuration is necessary if you are going to run the application programs frequently. Your computer will be able to deliver its peak performance in this configuration. The recommended RAM is also necessary if you intend to run more than one program at the same time.

The table below compares the minimum and recommended requirements of a very simple application program, a moderately complex program, and a very complex application program.

Program Name	The Sims	Word 2002	Via Voice 2000
Program Type	Video Game	Word Processor	Voice Dictation
Complexity Level	High	Medium	High
Microprocessor			
Minimum	Pentium/233	Pentium/266	Pentium II/300
Recommended	—	—	Pentium III/600
RAM			
Minimum	32 MB	20 MB	64 MB
Recommended	—	—	96 MB
Hard Drive Space			
Minimum	300 MB	147 MB	510 MB
Recommended	—	247 MB	—
Operating System			
Minimum	Windows 95 or later	Windows 98 or later	Windows 98 later Windows 2000
Recommended	—	—	—
Other Hardware			
Minimum	4x CD-ROM Drive, 2 MB video card	CD-ROM Drive	Sound Board, CD-ROM Drive, Microphone
Recommended	—	Modem	—

Setting Up a Computer

When you set up a computer, you can take specific measures to make your work and play more productive and comfortable. This section offers advice on setting up a computer and developing healthy work habits that can reduce the risk of discomfort or injury.

Ergonomics

Ergonomics is the science of designing the equipment we work with to maximize productivity and reduce fatigue. When you set up a computer system at your home or office, it is important to consider how you can sit and work at the computer as comfortably as possible. A few rules of thumb can help you arrange your computer workstation ergonomically.

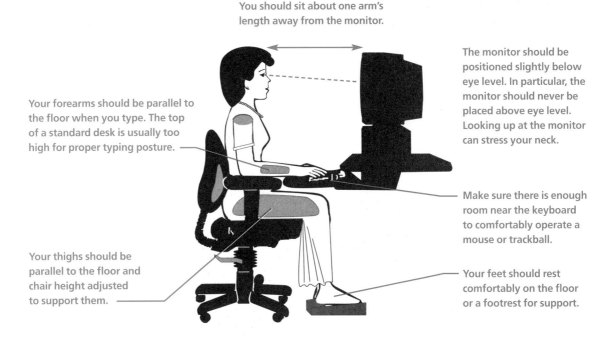

You should sit about one arm's length away from the monitor.

The monitor should be positioned slightly below eye level. In particular, the monitor should never be placed above eye level. Looking up at the monitor can stress your neck.

Your forearms should be parallel to the floor when you type. The top of a standard desk is usually too high for proper typing posture.

Make sure there is enough room near the keyboard to comfortably operate a mouse or trackball.

Your thighs should be parallel to the floor and chair height adjusted to support them.

Your feet should rest comfortably on the floor or a footrest for support.

Computer Furniture

Many stores carry furniture designed especially for computers. For example, certain desks equipped with keyboard drawers that place the keyboard at the optimal level for typing. If you expect to spend a great deal of time at the computer, good furniture is a sound investment in your health and comfort.

Photo courtesy of Computer Furniture Direct.

Your Chair

A high-quality chair is another key to working comfortably at the computer. It should have adjustments for the seat back and height. The chair should also give good support to your lower back. If the chair is equipped with arms, they should be adjustable.

An affordable alternative to an expensive computer chair is to purchase an ergonomic backrest instead. Backrests can save you 80% or more over the purchase of a chair.

See the Lesson 1 Web page for links to Web sites about computer-related ergonomics.

This backrest may give good support at 20% the cost of an equivalent chair.

Photos courtesy of Obusforme.

Healthy Work Habits with Computers

Operating any piece of equipment over a long period of time carries risks. The specific health risks posed by frequent computer operation are still being identified. Some of the risks under study are:

- radiation from computer monitors
- eye strain from full-time use
- repetitive stress injuries

Radiation Issues

Sit at least an arm's length away from the monitor.

All computer monitors emit radiation while in use. Computer monitors and television sets both use the same cathode ray tube (CRT) technology. However, computer monitors are built with much better shielding to reduce radiation. The amount of radiation emitted by computer monitors is not directly related to the size of the screen. In other words, a small, older monitor may emit more radiation than a new, larger one. Also, monitors put out more radiation from the sides and rear than from the front. Many manufacturers are designing new monitors that emit less radiation.

Eye Strain

Periodically focus your eyes across the room or out a window (a different distance from the monitor).

Some computer users have reported blurred vision after long work sessions in front of a monitor. This can be caused by staring at a fixed distance for long periods of time. Our eyes are used to focusing at various distances every few minutes.

Repetitive Stress Injuries

TIP!

If you think you are experiencing a repetitive stress injury, seek medical advice as early as possible.

Repetitive stress injuries (RSIs) can occur when the same motion is repeated over and over again for prolonged periods. If you are typing at a computer keyboard all day long, the muscles in your hands and wrists can become stressed. Some intense projects, such as graphic design, may require hundreds of motions each hour to maneuver the mouse and give commands from the keyboard.

Awareness is Key!

Awareness may be the best medicine to prevent the painful and debilitating effects of repetitive stress injuries. One symptom can be numbness and tingling sensations in the wrist, palm, or forearm. In a severe case, every motion of the affected area can become quite painful.

In recent years, there has been an increase in computer-related repetitive stress injuries, including tendonitis and carpal tunnel syndrome. This is a result of the widespread use of computers and the long hours people are working on them. These injuries are difficult to treat, so be careful and take preventive measures.

Preventive Measures

TIP!

See the Lesson 1 Web page for links to Web sites about computer-related health issues.

With good work habits, your risk of injury is greatly reduced. The following tips can help you avoid a repetitive stress injury, even if you work at a computer many hours each day.

- Take frequent rest breaks.

- Do hand-strengthening exercises (keep a squeeze ball near the computer).

- Maintain proper hand positioning at the keyboard; a wrist rest may help you.

- Invest in ergonomic computer furniture and hardware, including a comfortable chair, keyboard, and mouse.

- Apply an ice pack to your hand and wrist to help reduce inflammation, but see a doctor if any type of discomfort continues.

Concepts Review

True/False Questions

1. The primary chip on a personal computer system board is called a microprocessor.   TRUE   FALSE

2. A megabyte is larger than a gigabyte.   TRUE   FALSE

3. Software designed to help you get work done is called user data files.   TRUE   FALSE

4. A computer's RAM works just like the storage space on the hard drive.   TRUE   FALSE

5. The sharpness of a printer's output is measured by its resolution.   TRUE   FALSE

6. The latest, fastest microprocessor is always the best choice for a new computer.   TRUE   FALSE

7. The image you see on the computer's monitor (screen) is made up of pixels.   TRUE   FALSE

8. Floppy disks can hold just as much data as hard drives.   TRUE   FALSE

9. Software that controls the computer's basic functions is called an operating system.   TRUE   FALSE

10. Because they are much smaller, notebook computers generally cost less than desktop computers.   TRUE   FALSE

Multiple Choice Questions

1. Which statement best describes how you should shop for a new computer?
   a. Get the fastest computer available.
   b. Get a computer that meets the requirements of the application program you plan to use.
   c. Get the least expensive computer available.
   d. None of the above

2. Hardware components that are outside the system unit case are called:
   a. Accessories
   b. Printers and modems
   c. Pointing devices
   d. Peripherals

3. Among the health risks of working with computers are the following:
   a. Radiation
   b. Gamer's elbow
   c. Repetitive stress injury
   d. Eyestrain
   e. a, c, and d
   f. a, b, c, and d

4. The three primary types of software are:
   a. Anti-virus, user data, applications
   b. Applications, user data, operating system
   c. Operating system, word processor, spreadsheet
   d. Applications, utilities, operating system

Concept Matrix

Place a check mark in the correct column for each term:

Item	Hardware	Software
Modem	_____	_____
Windows XP	_____	_____
Printer	_____	_____
Floppy disk	_____	_____
Word processing application	_____	_____
Floppy drive	_____	_____
Letter document file	_____	_____
Computer system	_____	_____
Peripherals	_____	_____
Application program	_____	_____

Skill Builders

Skill Builder 1.1 Research Software Requirements

- Visit a store that sells computer software.

- Examine at least four software application programs you would like to run on your own computer. They should be programs that help you get useful work done in your job or as a hobby.

- Make notes on the system requirements of each software application program.

- Use these notes to create a basic requirements list for the computer system you will research in the next exercise.

Skill Builder 1.2 Research Your Own Computer System

Look up computer system advertisements in a local periodical or visit a local computer store. Determine the following information for at least two different systems:

- The model of microprocessor and its clock speed

- The system RAM

- The video RAM

- The capacity of the hard drive

- The size and type (CRT or LCD) of the video monitor, its dot pitch, and its resolution

Skill Builder 1.3 Make a Purchase Recommendation

Using the information presented in this lesson, write a specification for a system you would like to purchase for your use at home or work.

- Include any additional peripherals (such as a scanner or video capture card).

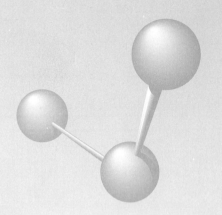

LESSON 2

Windows: Working with Windows Programs

As you learned in Lesson 1, the operating system is software that controls the basic functions of your computer. When you work with application programs such as those in the Office XP Suite, the Windows operating system controls your interactions with the programs and peripherals, such as the printer. This lesson introduces many basic techniques for working with Windows programs in Windows 95, Windows 98, Windows ME, and Windows 2000.

These techniques work with virtually any Windows program, not just the Office XP Suite. You will learn how to start programs, adjust the size of program windows, and how to run more than one program at once (multitasking). You will also learn the basics of saving your work and giving commands with menu bars and dialog boxes. By the end of this lesson, you should be able to work with the basic commands of almost any Windows application program.

See the Lesson 2 Web Page at: labpub.com/learn/bc/ccw/lesson2

Case Study

Michael has just purchased his first computer, a discount model that didn't set him back much but has all the features he needs. It isn't the fastest computer on the market, but Michael made sure it was powerful enough to run the basic types of programs he will use for the next couple of years. The only software that came with the computer was the operating system, Windows 98. But Michael discovers that Windows features several basic application programs called applets. When a friend asks Michael to help him put together a meeting announcement, he is eager to demonstrate what his computer and printer can do.

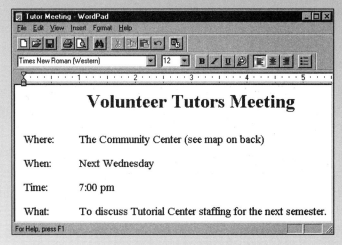

WordPad is a basic word processing application that you can use to type simple documents, like a one-page letter, with ease.

Michael's friend also wants to print a map with directions to the meeting, so he starts the Paint program and has soon drawn a map showing the location of the meeting.

The Paint applet is a simple drawing program. It features tools you use for drawing lines, boxes, circles, and text. It even has a spray paint tool.

Introducing Windows

Windows is an operating system. As you may recall from Lesson 1, there are three primary categories of software: the operating system, application programs, and user data files. As the operating system, Windows controls all the basic functions of the computer. Windows serves as the interface between you and the hardware and software that make up the computer system.

Roles of an Operating System

Windows plays several critical roles, such as those described below.

- **Managing file storage**—Windows controls the hard disk drives, floppy drive, and any other storage devices on the computer. For example, if you need to edit a letter you typed recently, Windows tells the computer system where the data for this letter is located and how to retrieve the letter into the word processing program for editing.

- **Managing Random Access Memory (RAM)**—As you learned in Lesson 1, your computer uses RAM as the "workbench" where all of your programs are run. Windows controls RAM and allocates it to the various application programs you run.

- **Managing Programs**—Windows is a multitasking operating system that allows several programs to run simultaneously. Windows manages the programs and ensures they have adequate RAM in which to run. Windows controls the interaction of each application program with other software and hardware. It also lets you switch between programs and copy information between them.

- **Managing Hardware and Peripherals**—Windows controls the hardware inside the system unit. For example, when you click with the mouse or tap a key on the keyboard, Windows receives your command and either executes it or passes the command on the application program you are running. Windows also controls the display of everything you see on the computer monitor. When you print a document, Windows sends the commands and data that tell the printer what to print.

Ease of Learning

Imagine if every make of car had its gas and brake pedals in a different location from other makes. Or if you had a turn signal control on the steering wheel in one make of car and on the left side of the dashboard in another. That's the way software was in the early days of personal computers (PCs). Learning one program did not necessarily help you learn the next one. Fortunately, this is no longer the case.

As you make your way through these lessons, you will learn basic commands and techniques that apply to virtually any Windows program you may encounter. This consistency is an important feature of Windows and of software that uses a Graphic User Interface (GUI). It makes learning how to use computers and various computer programs much easier than it was in the past. Computers were once the realm of programmers and specialists. Now, anyone can learn to use a computer effectively.

Switching On the Computer

You switch on the computer with a power switch on the front or side of the system unit. Most computers also have peripheral devices such as a printer or graphic scanner attached to the system unit. You should switch on these peripherals before you switch on the system unit. This ensures the system unit will recognize the peripherals as it "wakes up."

 ## Hands-On 2.1 Switching On the Computer

In many computer labs, the computers will already be switched on. If yours is not already on, use the steps in this exercise to power up the computer.

1. Remove any floppy disks from the floppy drive.
   The computer will not start properly if a floppy disk is in the drive. To eject a floppy disk, press the small button on the floppy drive.

2. If the computer is plugged into a surge protector, make sure the surge protector is switched on.

3. If there is a printer or scanner attached to the computer, switch on any of these devices.

4. Follow these steps to switch on the computer:

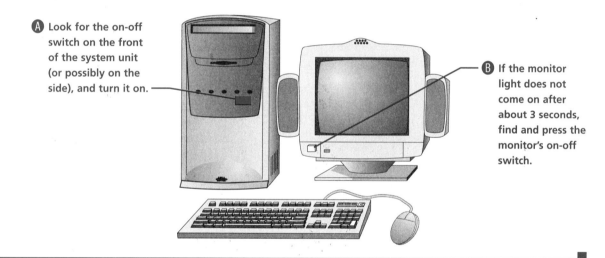

Ⓐ Look for the on-off switch on the front of the system unit (or possibly on the side), and turn it on.

Ⓑ If the monitor light does not come on after about 3 seconds, find and press the monitor's on-off switch.

Logging On to Windows

After the computer system completes its power-up routine, you may see a dialog box similar to the ones illustrated on the middle of page 44. The Enter Password and Enter Network Password dialog boxes prompt you to select or type a user name and password. A dialog box is one way to issue commands to Windows. Many home systems are set up to avoid the need to log on, but in most classrooms you will need to follow a log-on procedure.

Entering a User Name

Logging on requires you to select a user name. Your user name is important because it may give you a personal Desktop that can be customized. Also, your user name may restrict your access to devices such as printers. Your instructor will tell you which user name you should select in the following Hands-On exercise.

Hands-On 2.2 Logging On to Windows

In this exercise, you will log on to Windows by entering your username and password (if necessary). You can skip this exercise if your system does not require you to log on.

1. Get a user name and password from your instructor, and write them in the spaces below.

   User Name: _____   Password: _____   ❏ No password required

2. Find the dialog box below that matches your computer and follow the steps.
   Notice how asterisks represent the password you type. This prevents someone passing by from reading your password.

Ⓐ Hold down the (SHIFT) key as you tap the (TAB) key. You will see a highlight in the User Name box. Release the (SHIFT) key.

Ⓑ Type your user name here, then tap the (TAB) key to jump to the password box.

Ⓒ If necessary, enter your password.

Ⓐ Tap the ⬇ or ⬆ arrow keys on the keyboard until the bar highlights your user name. If your user name is not visible, just keep tapping the cursor key until it appears.

Ⓑ Tap the (TAB) key, then if necessary enter your password.

Windows XP

Ⓐ Tap and release the left mouse button (click) on your assigned user name.

Ⓑ Type your password if necessary.

3. Tap the (ENTER) key to log on.
   After a brief pause, the Windows Desktop will appear.

The Windows Desktop

After you log on, Windows will display the Desktop. Depending on how the computer is set up, Windows may also automatically run one or more programs. For example you may see an anti-virus program start running after the Desktop appears. The Desktop is the workspace in which you run programs in Windows. Your Desktop will look similar to the following illustration, but may differ in a few details.

Desktop icons provide access to frequently used Windows features.
Note: These items probably will not appear on the Windows XP Desktop.

Programs run in windows on the Desktop, or a program may cover the entire Desktop.

The Start button launches the main menu for running Windows programs.

The Quick Launch toolbar gives single-click access to programs. Note: This item will not appear on the Windows XP Taskbar.

The taskbar helps you switch between programs.

The System Tray displays icons for system services running in the background, such as the system time clock.

Displaying the Desktop without Logging On

It is often possible to display the Desktop without actually logging on. Windows usually displays a default (generic) Desktop whenever the Cancel button is clicked on the log-on dialog box. However, you may not have access to the normal command menus or printers in the lab if you use this method. It is best to log on with your assigned user name. Some networked computers in offices won't let you get to the Desktop at all without a user name and password.

Using a Mouse

You will give most of your commands to Windows with a mouse. A mouse is a pointing device. It lets you point to various screen locations and issue commands. The mouse was invented in 1963 by Douglas Englebart, a Stanford University professor. It probably got its name from the tail-like cable that connects it to the computer. If you have never used a mouse before, this lesson—and the ones to follow—will give you plenty of practice.

Mouse Buttons

A typical mouse has two buttons for issuing commands. Some mice have three buttons in which the middle button has various functions, depending on the program being used. The two main mouse buttons are shown below, along with the proper way to grasp the mouse in your hand.

TIP!

Windows allows you to reverse the right and left mouse buttons. Left-handed users often select this option. Open the Mouse icon in the Windows control panel to see this option. You will do this in the next Hands-On exercise.

Primary button: The left mouse button is the one used most frequently. Most commands are issued with this button.

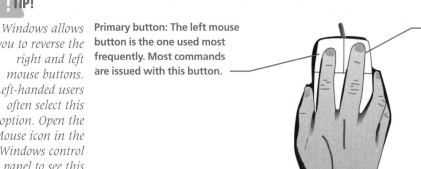

Secondary button: The right, or secondary button, often displays a special pop-up menu.

You can perform five basic motions with a mouse. Each motion has specific uses in Windows and application programs.

QUICK REFERENCE: MOUSE MOTIONS

Motion Name	How to Do It
Click	Gently tap and immediately release the primary (left) mouse button. You use this motion to give most commands.
Double-click	Click the primary button twice in rapid succession. This motion is usually a shortcut to open an object on the screen.
Drag	Press and hold down the primary mouse button while you slide the mouse to a new location. Release the mouse button when you reach the destination. This motion is usually used to move objects on the screen.
Right-click	Gently tap and immediately release the secondary (right) mouse button. This is usually used to display special menus.
Point	Slide the mouse without pressing a button until the pointer is in the desired location.

Pointing with the Mouse

When you point with the mouse, you should always remember that the tip of the arrow is the spot at which you are pointing. You want to make sure that the tip of the arrow touches any menu or button that you wish to click.

The pointer is too high.

The pointer is too low.

The pointer is just right.

Hands-On 2.3 Use the Mouse

In this exercise, you will practice pointing and clicking. You will see the difference between a normal click and a right-click on the Start button.

1. Follow the steps below for the version of Windows you are using.

Windows 98, NT, ME, and 2000

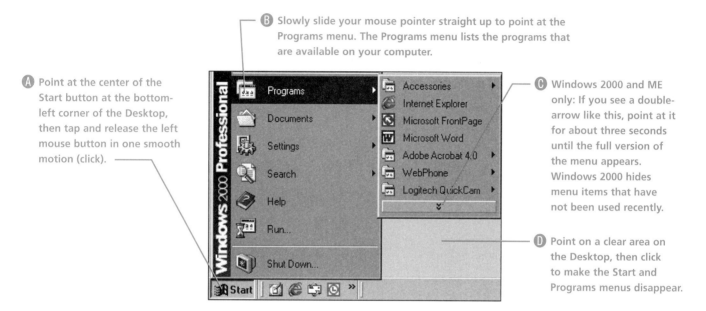

Ⓑ Slowly slide your mouse pointer straight up to point at the Programs menu. The Programs menu lists the programs that are available on your computer.

Ⓐ Point at the center of the Start button at the bottom-left corner of the Desktop, then tap and release the left mouse button in one smooth motion (click).

Ⓒ Windows 2000 and ME only: If you see a double-arrow like this, point at it for about three seconds until the full version of the menu appears. Windows 2000 hides menu items that have not been used recently.

Ⓓ Point on a clear area on the Desktop, then click to make the Start and Programs menus disappear.

Windows XP

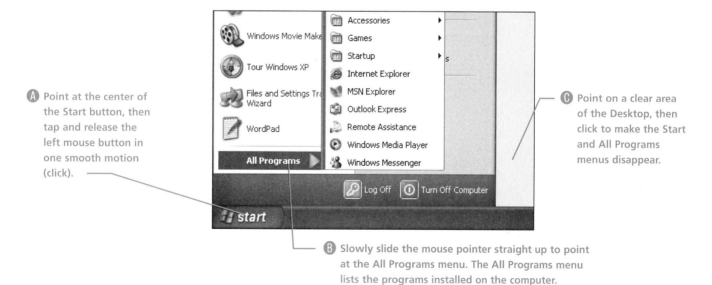

Ⓐ Point at the center of the Start button, then tap and release the left mouse button in one smooth motion (click).

Ⓒ Point on a clear area of the Desktop, then click to make the Start and All Programs menus disappear.

Ⓑ Slowly slide the mouse pointer straight up to point at the All Programs menu. The All Programs menu lists the programs installed on the computer.

(Continued on the next page)

2. Follow these steps to practice a right-click:

Ⓐ Point at the Start button, but this time tap and release the right mouse button (a right-click). You will see a pop-up menu appear.

Ⓑ Point and click with the left (not the right) mouse button on a clear area on the Desktop to make the pop-up menu disappear.

Practice Double-Clicking and Dragging

Windows lets you adjust the speed of the double-click mouse motion. In the next steps of this exercise, you will practice adjusting the double-click speed.

3. Follow the steps below for the version of Windows you are running:

Windows 98, NT, ME, and 2000

Ⓐ Click Start.   Ⓑ Click Settings.   Ⓒ Click Control Panel.

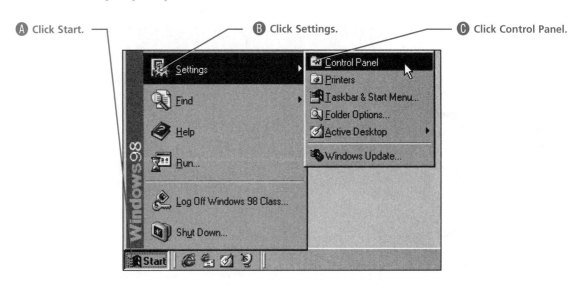

Ⓓ Look for the Mouse icon. If you do not see it, tap the Ⓜ key on the keyboard two or three times until it comes into view.

Windows XP Only:
If you do not see a mouse icon like the one shown here, click the View All Control Panel options link on the left side of the Control Panel window.

Ⓔ Click on the Mouse icon with the right (not the left) button, then slide the pointer down and click on the Open command in the pop-up menu. Continue with Step 4 on the following page.

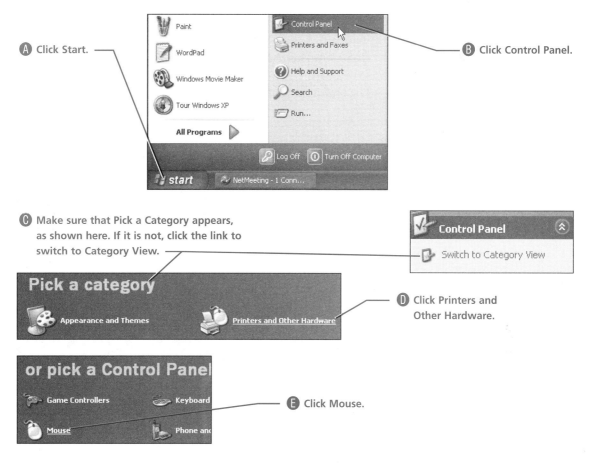

Ⓐ Click Start.

Ⓑ Click Control Panel.

Ⓒ Make sure that Pick a Category appears, as shown here. If it is not, click the link to switch to Category View.

Ⓓ Click Printers and Other Hardware.

Ⓔ Click Mouse.

The Mouse options window will now be displayed.

4. Follow these steps to adjust the double-click speed of the mouse:
Note: In Windows XP, the test area features a folder rather than a jack-in-the-box.

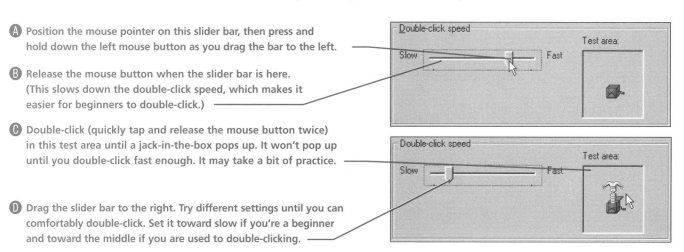

Ⓐ Position the mouse pointer on this slider bar, then press and hold down the left mouse button as you drag the bar to the left.

Ⓑ Release the mouse button when the slider bar is here. (This slows down the double-click speed, which makes it easier for beginners to double-click.)

Ⓒ Double-click (quickly tap and release the mouse button twice) in this test area until a jack-in-the-box pops up. It won't pop up until you double-click fast enough. It may take a bit of practice.

Ⓓ Drag the slider bar to the right. Try different settings until you can comfortably double-click. Set it toward slow if you're a beginner and toward the middle if you are used to double-clicking.

5. Click the OK button at the bottom of the Mouse options window to close the window.

6. Click the Close ⊠ button at the very top-right corner of the Control Panel window to close that window.

Starting Programs

You can start a program by clicking the Start  button and choosing the desired program from the Programs menu. You can also start a program by double-clicking a Desktop icon for the program (if a Desktop icon exists). For example, the Internet Explorer Web browser program typically has a Desktop icon. Also, you can launch some programs from the Quick Launch toolbar that is next to the Start button.

Internet Explorer

 !NOTE!

Windows XP does contain the Quick Launch toolbar feature.

The Quick Launch toolbar lets you start programs with a single click.

Hands-On 2.4 Start WordPad

In this exercise, you will use the Start menu to launch the WordPad program. WordPad is an entry-level word processing program you can use to create letters and other simple documents. In a later exercise, you will use WordPad to compose a meeting announcement.

1. Follow the steps below for the version of Windows you are running:

Windows 98, NT, ME, and 2000

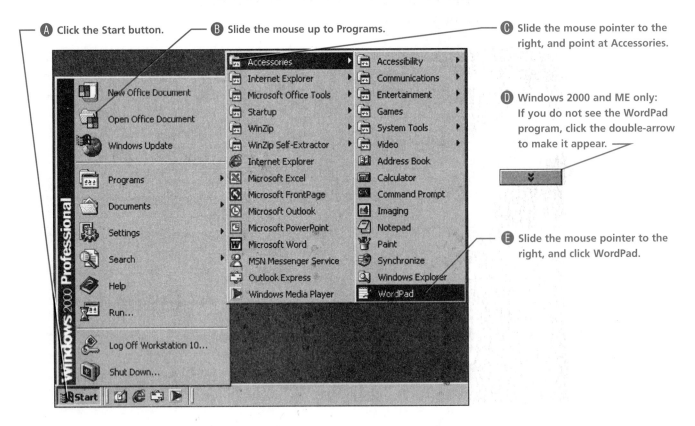

Ⓐ Click the Start button.

Ⓑ Slide the mouse up to Programs.

Ⓒ Slide the mouse pointer to the right, and point at Accessories.

Ⓓ Windows 2000 and ME only: If you do not see the WordPad program, click the double-arrow to make it appear.

Ⓔ Slide the mouse pointer to the right, and click WordPad.

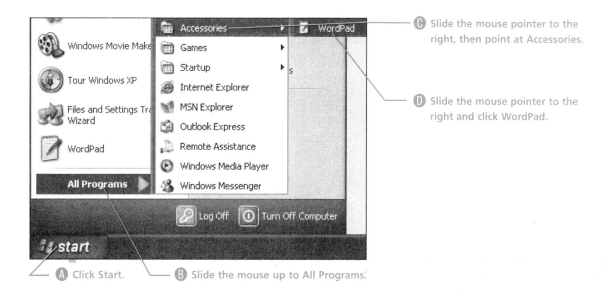

C Slide the mouse pointer to the right, then point at Accessories.

D Slide the mouse pointer to the right and click WordPad.

A Click Start.

B Slide the mouse up to All Programs.

The WordPad program window appears on the Desktop.

Elements of a Program Window

Every program runs in its own program window. The WordPad window you have open now is a good example of a typical Windows program. Since the controls in most program windows work similarly, once you have mastered a program such as WordPad, you are well on your way to mastering Windows programs in general. Take a few moments to look over the common features shown in the following illustration.

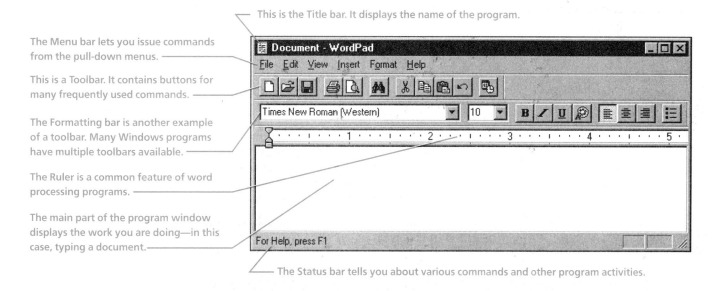

This is the Title bar. It displays the name of the program.

The Menu bar lets you issue commands from the pull-down menus.

This is a Toolbar. It contains buttons for many frequently used commands.

The Formatting bar is another example of a toolbar. Many Windows programs have multiple toolbars available.

The Ruler is a common feature of word processing programs.

The main part of the program window displays the work you are doing—in this case, typing a document.

The Status bar tells you about various commands and other program activities.

Sizing Program Windows

You can control the position and size of program windows on the Desktop. For example, you may want a program window to occupy the entire Desktop or you may want two or more program windows displayed side-by-side.

Quick Sizing Buttons

Every program window displays quick sizing buttons at the top-right corners that allow you to give the most common window commands with a single click. The following table describes the function of each quick sizing button.

Button	Description
Minimize	Removes the program window from the Desktop but keeps the program running. Clicking the program button on the Taskbar restores the program window.
Maximize	Expands the program window until it covers the entire Desktop. Only the maximized program and the Taskbar are visible.
Restore	Restores a program window to the size it was set to before it was maximized. A restored window usually covers only a portion of the Desktop.
Close	Closes a document window or exits a program.

The Switching Restore and Maximize Buttons

The Maximize and Restore buttons never appear together. Instead, when either button is clicked, the window changes and displays the other button, as shown in the example below:

When you click the maximize button here . . .

. . . the middle button displays the restore button . . .

. . . and if you click the restore button . . .

. . . it changes back to the maximize button.

 ## Hands-On 2.5 Use the Quick Sizing Buttons

In this exercise, you will practice using the Minimize, Maximize, Restore, and Close quick sizing Buttons.

1. Notice the WordPad ![Document - WordPad] button near the Start button on the Taskbar.
   The button is recessed (pushed in) because WordPad is the active program. A button appears on the Taskbar for each running program.

2. Look at the top-right corner of the WordPad window and notice the three quick sizing buttons.
   If the window is already maximized, then the Restore button will be displayed in the center of the trio. If the last WordPad user sized the window to cover just part of the Desktop, then the Maximize button will be displayed.

3. If the middle quick sizing button is the Maximize ![button] button, then click it.
   At this point, the WordPad window will be maximized. Only the WordPad window, the Taskbar, and the Start button should be visible.

4. Click the Minimize ![button] button on the WordPad window.
   The window vanishes, but the WordPad button is still visible on the Taskbar.

5. Click the WordPad ![Document - WordPad] button on the Taskbar and the window will reappear.
   You can always restore a minimized window by clicking that program's button on the Taskbar.

6. Click the Restore ![Restore] button, and the window will occupy only part of the Desktop.
   Leave the WordPad window open.

Moving Program Windows

You can move a window on the Desktop to various screen locations by dragging on its title bar. The only time you cannot move a window is if it is maximized. You can tell when a window is maximized because it will have a Restore quick sizing button.

Changing the Size of a Program Window

You can adjust the size and shape of an open window by dragging the window's borders. When you point to the border of a window that is restored (i.e., not maximized), you will see a double-arrow appear. The arrows will point in the directions you can resize the window.

Tip: You cannot change the size of a maximized window.

See the Web page for this lesson to view a video on sizing program windows.

Hands-On 2.6 Move and Size the WordPad Window

In this exercise, you will move the WordPad window to a different location on the Desktop, then change the size of the window.

1. Follow these steps to move the WordPad window:

NOTE!   *It's OK if your WordPad window has different dimensions than shown below.*

Windows XP users will probably not see My Computer and Network Neighborhood icons on the Desktop. These are now found in the Start menu.

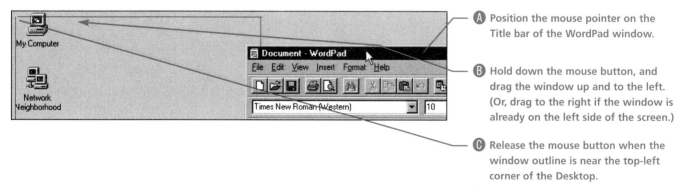

Ⓐ Position the mouse pointer on the Title bar of the WordPad window.

Ⓑ Hold down the mouse button, and drag the window up and to the left. (Or, drag to the right if the window is already on the left side of the screen.)

Ⓒ Release the mouse button when the window outline is near the top-left corner of the Desktop.

2. Drag on the title bar of the WordPad window again, but this time drag down toward the bottom-right of the Desktop.

3. Drag the title bar once more to place the WordPad window at the top-center of the Desktop.

(Continued on the next page)

4. Follow these steps to change the size of the WordPad window:

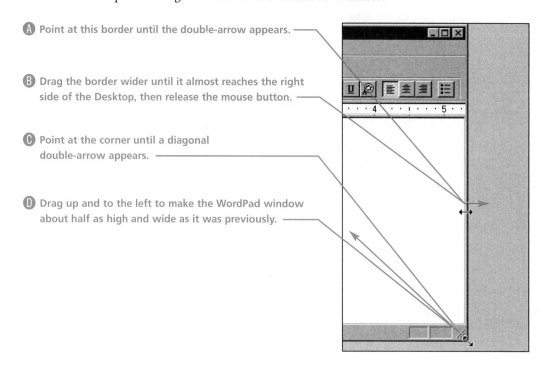

Ⓐ Point at this border until the double-arrow appears.

Ⓑ Drag the border wider until it almost reaches the right side of the Desktop, then release the mouse button.

Ⓒ Point at the corner until a diagonal double-arrow appears.

Ⓓ Drag up and to the left to make the WordPad window about half as high and wide as it was previously.

5. Change only the height of the window by dragging the bottom border up or down.

6. Practice some more until you can place and size the WordPad window at any desired location on the Desktop.
   This skill will become very useful when you run more than one program at once and need to arrange them on the Desktop so you can see the contents of one window as you work in a different window.

7. When you are finished, maximize 🗖 the WordPad window.
   It is often easier to work in a maximized window, because it covers any distracting elements that may be on the Desktop.

Working with Programs

Application programs such as WordPad are designed to help you get work done on the computer. Thousands of application programs are available to help you accomplish a wide variety of tasks. Many of the techniques you use to work with the WordPad program in these exercises will apply to other Windows programs as well. Most programs let you give commands with pull-down menus, toolbars, and keyboard shortcuts. You will use all three types of commands in the Hands-On exercises in this lesson.

Using Toolbars

WordPad's toolbars include buttons for the most frequently used commands. Most of these buttons are either toggles that you switch on and off, or have drop-down lists from which you make a selection.

This toolbar button issues the Print command. ——

A click on this button activates the Bold command. Notice how the button appears to be "pressed" when compared to the button next to it. ——

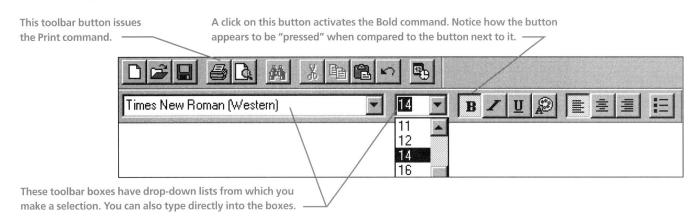

These toolbar boxes have drop-down lists from which you make a selection. You can also type directly into the boxes. ——

Hands-On 2.7 Type a Meeting Announcement

In this exercise, you will use some of WordPad's toolbar commands as you type a simple meeting announcement. The commands you will use let you change the look of the text in the document.

Format and Type a Heading

1. Tap the (ENTER) key six times to add space to the top margin of the announcement.
   Each time you tap the (ENTER) key in a word processing document, you add a new line to the document. Each new line is usually about one-sixth of an inch high.

2. Follow these steps to set the format for the announcement heading:

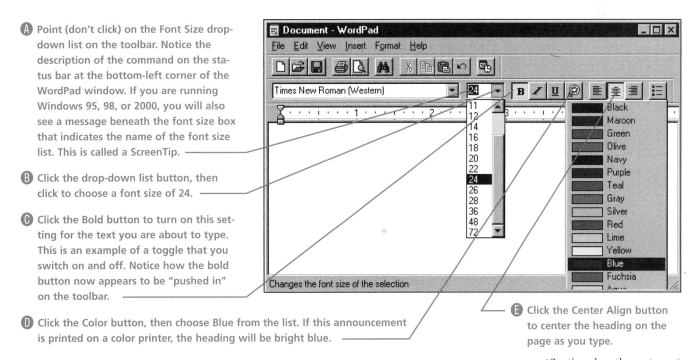

Ⓐ Point (don't click) on the Font Size drop-down list on the toolbar. Notice the description of the command on the status bar at the bottom-left corner of the WordPad window. If you are running Windows 95, 98, or 2000, you will also see a message beneath the font size box that indicates the name of the font size list. This is called a ScreenTip. ——

Ⓑ Click the drop-down list button, then click to choose a font size of 24. ——

Ⓒ Click the Bold button to turn on this setting for the text you are about to type. This is an example of a toggle that you switch on and off. Notice how the bold button now appears to be "pushed in" on the toolbar. ——

Ⓓ Click the Color button, then choose Blue from the list. If this announcement is printed on a color printer, the heading will be bright blue. ——

Ⓔ Click the Center Align button to center the heading on the page as you type.

(Continued on the next page)

3. Type the heading for the announcement: **Volunteer Tutors Meeting**
   The size and color of the letters will match the settings you made in the previous step.

4. Tap the (ENTER) key on the keyboard twice to add space between the heading and the body of the announcement that you are about to type.

Format and Type the Body of the Announcement

5. Follow these steps to format the body text of the announcement:

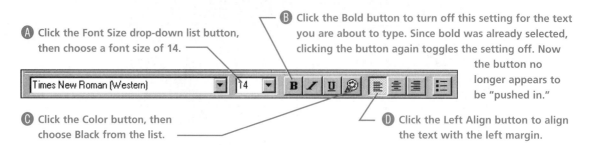

Ⓐ Click the Font Size drop-down list button, then choose a font size of 14.

Ⓑ Click the Bold button to turn off this setting for the text you are about to type. Since bold was already selected, clicking the button again toggles the setting off. Now the button no longer appears to be "pushed in."

Ⓒ Click the Color button, then choose Black from the list.

Ⓓ Click the Left Align button to align the text with the left margin.

6. Follow these steps to type the body of the announcement:

Ⓐ Type **Where:** and then tap the (TAB) key.

Ⓑ Type **The Community Center (see map on back)**, then tap the (ENTER) key twice to create a double space.

Ⓒ Continue typing the rest of the announcement. You may need to tap the (TAB) key twice after Time and What to make these lines even with the first two lines.

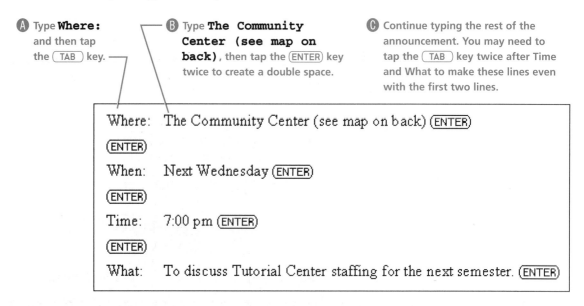

Leave the WordPad document open. You will use it again in a moment.

Using Pull-Down Menus

You use pull-down menus frequently in Windows programs to initiate commands. Almost all Windows programs use pull-down menus. Several symbols that appear on pull-down menus. You should be familiar with. The following illustration displays significant features in WordPad's File menu.

When you click a command with three dots after it, a dialog box with additional choices will be displayed. The three dots are called an ellipsis.

This command has a keyboard shortcut you can use to issue the command by holding down the first key and then tapping the second key.

WordPad stores a list of the most recently saved documents here. This makes it easier to open a document you just worked on.

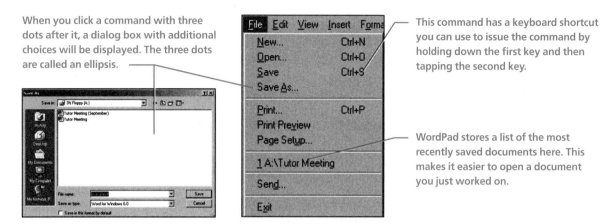

 ## Hands-On 2.8 Issue a Command from the Menu Bar

In this exercise, you will work with menu bar to access the Print Preview feature of WordPad..

1. Follow these steps to issue a command from the menu bar:

A Click the File command on the menu bar.

B Click the Print Preview command in the drop-down menu.

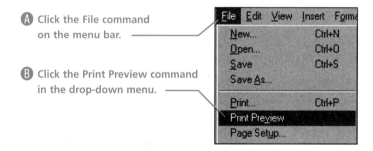

In the rest of this book, a command like this will be written File→Print Preview.

A preview of the printed page will appear in the WordPad window. This displays exactly how your document will appear when it is printed. The dashed lines indicate the margins of the document and will not appear in print.

2. Click the **Close** button on the top-right side of the WordPad window. *This closes the Print Preview window. Now you are back in normal document view.*

Saving Files

You create documents by using application programs like WordPad. The word file refers to any document that has been saved onto a storage device. A typical hard disk drive has thousands of files stored on it. With most Windows programs, you use the Save command to save your work in a file.

Where Your Work Takes Place

Many beginners think that what they see on the computer's monitor is taking place in the hard drive or on a floppy disk. This is not the case. As you use an application program, your work is placed in the computer's random access memory (RAM; see page 9) and is displayed on the monitor. However, RAM is erased when the power is switched off or when the system is restarted. This is why you must save your work on a floppy disk, hard disk, or other storage media if you want to save it for later use.

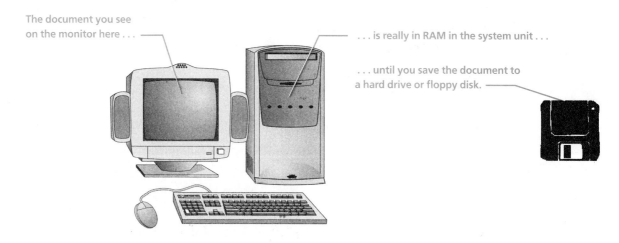

The document you see on the monitor here . . .

. . . is really in RAM in the system unit . . .

. . . until you save the document to a hard drive or floppy disk.

The Save and Save As Commands

FROM THE KEYBOARD

 (CTRL)+(S) to Save the current file.

Most Windows programs provide two commands that let you save documents. The File→Save command saves the current document onto a disk. If the document had previously been saved, then the old version is replaced by the new edited version. If the document is new, then a *Save As* dialog box appears. This allows you to name the document and specify the disk drive and folder to which you wish to save the document. You can also use the File→Save As command to make a copy of an existing document by saving the document with a new name.

VIDEO 2

See the Web page for this lesson to view a video saving a file to a floppy disk.

Naming Files

When you save a file for the first time, you must give it a name. Windows has specific rules for naming files. The following Quick Reference table lists the rules for naming files.

QUICK REFERENCE: RULES FOR FILE NAMES

Rule	Description
Filename length	A filename can contain up to 255 characters.
Characters that are allowed in filenames	A filename may contain numbers, spaces, periods, commas, semicolons, dashes, and parentheses.
Characters that are not allowed in filenames	A filename cannot contain the following characters: \ / : * ? " < > |.

Hands-On 2.9 Save the Announcement

In this exercise, you will save the WordPad document that is currently in RAM to your floppy disk.

1. Insert your exercise diskette into the floppy drive. The disk should be placed with the label side facing up and the metal plate facing in.
   If you are not sure how to insert a floppy disk, ask for assistance.

2. Follow these steps to issue the Save command:

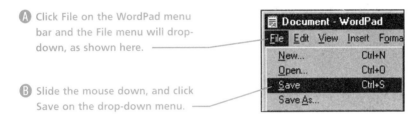

Ⓐ Click File on the WordPad menu bar and the File menu will drop-down, as shown here.

Ⓑ Slide the mouse down, and click Save on the drop-down menu.

3. Follow these steps to finish saving the document to your floppy disk:

Ⓐ Click the Save in drop-down list, and choose the 3½ Floppy (A:) drive.

Ⓑ Notice that WordPad proposes the name Document (or Document.doc) in the filename field.

Ⓒ Click in the Filename box to the right of the name Document. Use the (BACKSPACE) key on the keyboard to delete the name Document, and then type the name **Tutor Meeting** as shown here.

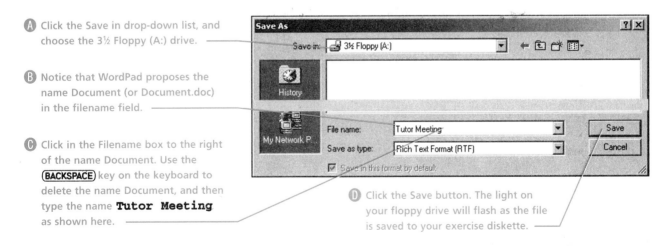

Ⓓ Click the Save button. The light on your floppy drive will flash as the file is saved to your exercise diskette.

Notice that the new name of your document is now displayed on the title bar at the top-left corner of the WordPad window.

Closing Program Windows

FROM THE KEYBOARD

ALT + F4 to close the active program window.

When you are finished working with a program, you will usually want to close the program window. This not only removes clutter from the Desktop, it also conserves RAM so you can run other programs more efficiently. Virtually all Windows programs have a File→Exit command you can use to close the program window. You can also close a program window with the Close quick sizing button at the top-right corner of the window.

 Hands-On 2.10 **Close WordPad**

In this exercise, you will close WordPad using commands on the menu bar.

1. Choose File→Exit from the menu bar. Click No if you are asked if you wish to save your document.
   The program window will close. If you type something in the document after issuing a Save command, WordPad asks if you wish to save the changes. In this case, there is no need to save the change.

Editing Files

After you have typed a document, it is easy to make changes. For example, let's say that another volunteer tutors meeting is to take place next month. Rather than typing the document again from scratch, you can simply change some of the information, then save the document again.

Working on a Previously Saved File

If you want to work on a previously saved file, you must open it in the application program. After you have changed the file, you have two ways to save your changes:

- **Save**—This command overwrites the old version of the file with the new version you have just edited.

- **Save As**—This command allows you to create a new file with the changes you have made, leaving the old version intact with the old filename.

 Hands-On 2.11 **Open and Edit a File**

In this exercise, you will open the meeting announcement you created earlier, edit it, then save the announcement with a new name.

Open the Meeting Announcement File

1. Click the Start button, then slide the mouse pointer up to the Programs menu (or All Programs if you are running Windows XP).

2. Slide the mouse pointer to the right, then up to Accessories, and then click the WordPad program at the bottom of the menu.

3. If the WordPad window is not already maximized, click the Maximize ▫ quick sizing button to make the WordPad window cover the Desktop.

4. Click the Open 📂 button on the WordPad toolbar.

5. Follow these steps to open the announcement file you saved to your floppy disk:

Ⓐ Click on the Look in drop-down list, then choose the 3½ Floppy (A:) drive.

Ⓑ Click on the Tutor Meeting file to select it for the Open command.

Ⓒ Notice that the name of the file is now listed in the Filename box.

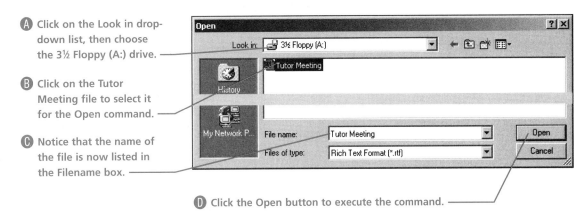

Ⓓ Click the Open button to execute the command.

You will see the floppy drive light flash as the file is loaded from the floppy drive into the computer's RAM. After it is loaded into RAM, the announcement document will be displayed in the WordPad window.

Edit the Meeting Announcement Document

6. Follow these steps to change the date for the meeting:

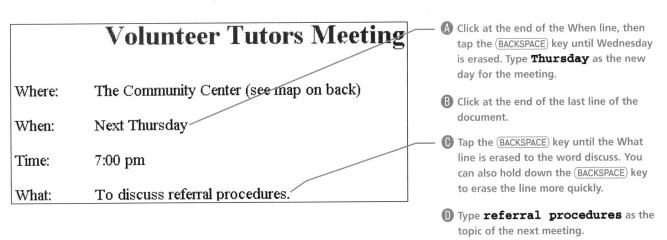

Ⓐ Click at the end of the When line, then tap the (BACKSPACE) key until Wednesday is erased. Type **Thursday** as the new day for the meeting.

Ⓑ Click at the end of the last line of the document.

Ⓒ Tap the (BACKSPACE) key until the What line is erased to the word discuss. You can also hold down the (BACKSPACE) key to erase the line more quickly.

Ⓓ Type **referral procedures** as the topic of the next meeting.

7. Choose File→Save As from the menu bar.

(Continued on the next page)

8. Follow these steps to save the file with a new name:

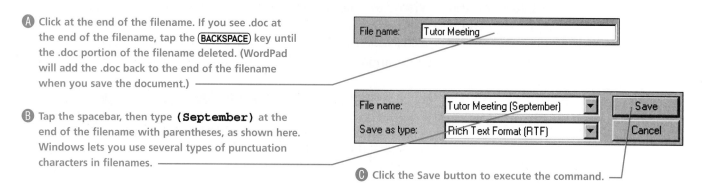

Ⓐ Click at the end of the filename. If you see .doc at the end of the filename, tap the (BACKSPACE) key until the .doc portion of the filename deleted. (WordPad will add the .doc back to the end of the filename when you save the document.)

Ⓑ Tap the spacebar, then type **(September)** at the end of the filename with parentheses, as shown here. Windows lets you use several types of punctuation characters in filenames.

Ⓒ Click the Save button to execute the command.

Now two versions of the announcement are saved to your floppy disk. The first version has not been changed.

9. Click the Restore 🗗 button at the top-right corner of the WordPad window. *Now WordPad occupies just a portion of the Desktop.*

Multitasking

One of the most useful features of Windows is the ability to run multiple programs simultaneously. This is known as multitasking. For example, you can download files from the Internet, print a long document, and type a letter in a word processor all at the same time. You click program buttons on the Taskbar to switch between multitasked programs.

How Many Programs Can You Multitask?

The number of programs you can run at the same time depends on how much RAM is installed on your computer. The more RAM you have, the more programs you can run efficiently at the same time. Large and complex programs require more RAM than simple programs. If you try to run more than one large program on a computer with a small amount of RAM, Windows will run much more slowly.

See the Web page for this lesson to view a video on multitasking.

 Hands-On 2.12 Start Paint

In this exercise, you will start a second program to run simultaneously with WordPad. Paint is a simple drawing program that comes with Windows.

1. Click the Start button, then point at the Programs (or All Programs) menu.

2. Slide the mouse pointer over to choose the Accessories menu, then click the Paint program. If you are using Windows 2000 or ME and you do not see the Paint program in the Accessories menu, click the Expand Menu ![⌄] command to make the entire menu appear.
The Paint program will launch.

3. If Paint is not already maximized, click the maximize button.
Paint's program window now covers the entire Desktop. However, you can see from the two buttons on the Taskbar that WordPad is still running. Since you just started Paint, it is now the active program. Notice how Paint's button on the Taskbar appears "pushed in" compared to the WordPad button.

Switching between Windows

When you run multiple programs, only one program window at a time can be active. The other program windows are inactive. You use the Taskbar to switch between the programs you are running. As you did in a previous exercise, you also use the Taskbar to restore a minimized program window.

Hands-On 2.13 Switch between Paint and WordPad

In this exercise, you will practice making WordPad and Paint the active program.

1. Click the [🗐 Tutor Meeting (September)...] button on the Taskbar to activate the WordPad program.
   Now WordPad's Taskbar button appears "pushed in." Notice also that WordPad's title bar has a different color than the title bar for the Paint window.

2. Click the [🖌 untitled - Paint] button on the Taskbar.
   That's all there is to switching from one program to another. The Paint window now appears on top of the WordPad window.

3. Click the Restore 🗗 button on the Paint window.
   Now Paint's window occupies just a portion of the Desktop.

4. If the WordPad window is not visible, point at the title bar on the Paint window, then drag the Paint window to a new position on the Desktop so that both windows are partially visible. For example, drag the title bar down and to the right.

The Paint window title bar ——

5. Click anywhere in the WordPad window to activate it.
   Whenever you click in a program window, it becomes the active program.

6. Click the Close ☒ button on the WordPad window to exit the program. Click Yes if WordPad asks you to save changes to the document.

7. Click the Maximize button on the Paint window.
   Leave the Paint window open, since you will begin drawing in a moment.

Using Dialog Boxes

Dialog boxes allow you to set options and controls for a command. You will encounter a variety of controls in dialog boxes. You used a dialog box earlier in this lesson to adjust the speed of double-clicks with the mouse. The following illustrations describe several common types of dialog box controls.

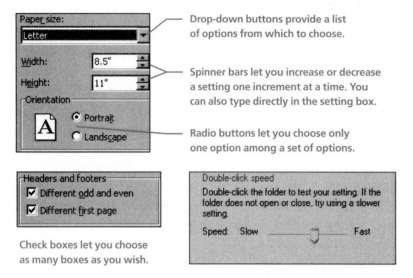

Drop-down buttons provide a list of options from which to choose.

Spinner bars let you increase or decrease a setting one increment at a time. You can also type directly in the setting box.

Radio buttons let you choose only one option among a set of options.

Check boxes let you choose as many boxes as you wish.

Slider bars let you adjust a setting by dragging a bar, as you did in a previous exercise.

 Hands-On 2.14 **Specify the Drawing Size**

In this exercise, you will use a dialog box to specify the size of your drawing. The options you set will reduce the size of the Paint file that you will save to your exercise diskette. This is necessary because the Paint program produces graphic files. Graphic files occupy a large amount of disk space when compared to text files. One Paint file can occupy your entire diskette if you do not make the settings defined in this exercise.

1. Click Image on the Paint menu bar.
   Notice that the Attributes command has three dots (ellipses) after its name. This indicates that this command uses a dialog box.

2. Click the Attributes command.
   You will use this dialog box to specify the drawing size. The drawing size also affects the size of the file when you save this drawing.

3. Follow these steps to set the drawing size (be sure to complete the steps in order: A, B, C, etc.):

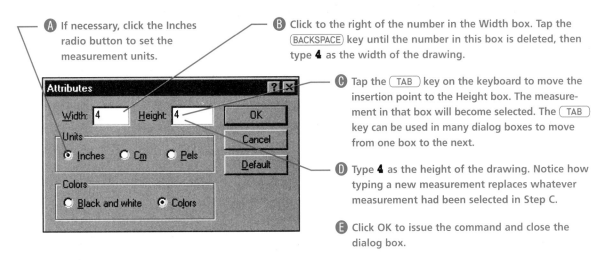

Ⓐ If necessary, click the Inches radio button to set the measurement units.

Ⓑ Click to the right of the number in the Width box. Tap the (BACKSPACE) key until the number in this box is deleted, then type **4** as the width of the drawing.

Ⓒ Tap the (TAB) key on the keyboard to move the insertion point to the Height box. The measurement in that box will become selected. The (TAB) key can be used in many dialog boxes to move from one box to the next.

Ⓓ Type **4** as the height of the drawing. Notice how typing a new measurement replaces whatever measurement had been selected in Step C.

Ⓔ Click OK to issue the command and close the dialog box.

The image size is set to 4″ by 4″. In the next few steps, you will save the empty drawing to your exercise diskette. You will use a drop-down button on the Save As dialog box to set the Save As Type. Most programs have a Save As Type option that lets you specify the type of file you wish to create. In the Paint program, you use the Save As Type option to determine the amount of color information that is stored in the file. You will reduce the amount of color information to conserve space on your diskette.

4. Choose File→Save from the menu bar.

5. Follow these steps to set the image file type for your drawing:

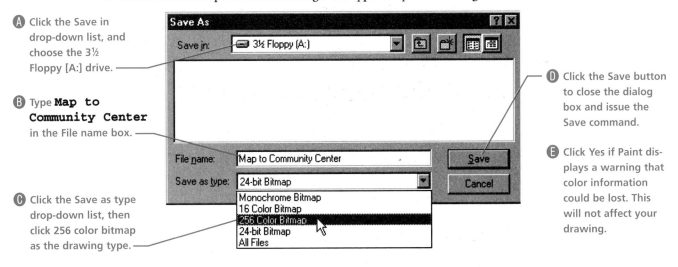

Ⓐ Click the Save in drop-down list, and choose the 3½ Floppy [A:] drive.

Ⓑ Type **Map to Community Center** in the File name box.

Ⓒ Click the Save as type drop-down list, then click 256 color bitmap as the drawing type.

Ⓓ Click the Save button to close the dialog box and issue the Save command.

Ⓔ Click Yes if Paint displays a warning that color information could be lost. This will not affect your drawing.

Working with the Paint Program

Paint is a small application (called an applet) that is bundled with Windows. Paint lets you use a mouse to create drawings and graphic images. Paint is known as a "bit map" program because images are formed by turning dots (called pixels) on and off on the screen. The dots are too tiny to see when printed. However, you can see them if you zoom in on the Paint screen.

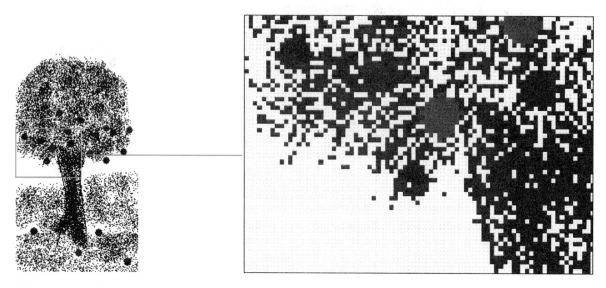

This tree is actually made up of numerous dots (pixels).

A close-up view of the tree drawing.

Using Tools from a Toolbox

Drawing programs often have a toolbox with buttons that represent the various drawing tools. Most toolboxes are designed as floating palettes you can position anywhere on the screen. Paint's toolbox has several tools that are also featured in more sophisticated drawing programs. The illustration to the right shows several of Paint's basic tools.

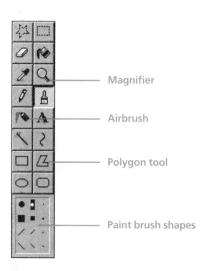

Magnifier

Airbrush

Polygon tool

Paint brush shapes

ScreenTips

Like many Windows programs, Paint's toolbox has a feature called ScreenTips. When you point at a button in Paint's toolbox for about two seconds, Paint will display a small box with the name of the tool.

 NOTE!   *The Windows NT version of Paint does not have the ScreenTips feature.*

Hands-On 2.15 Draw a Map

In this exercise, you will use several of Paint's tools to draw a simple map. When you are finished, you will save the drawing. Before you begin, take a look at the map on page 69 to see what the final version of the map will look like.

1. Follow these steps to draw lines for the streets on the map:

 TIP!   *The (SHIFT) key helps you to draw perfectly straight lines.*

Ⓐ Select the Line tool from the toolbox.

Ⓑ Select the thickness of the lines you will draw.

Ⓒ Select a dark color for the lines.

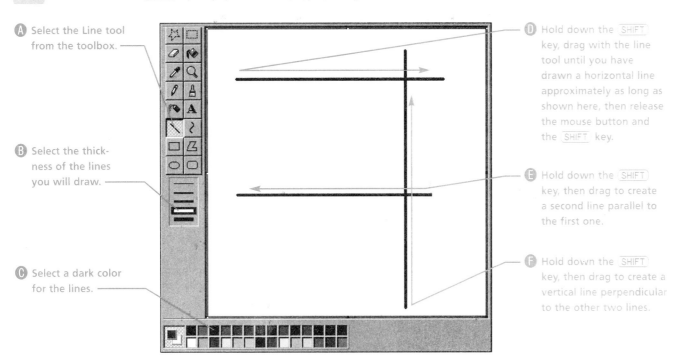

Ⓓ Hold down the (SHIFT) key, drag with the line tool until you have drawn a horizontal line approximately as long as shown here, then release the mouse button and the (SHIFT) key.

Ⓔ Hold down the (SHIFT) key, then drag to create a second line parallel to the first one.

Ⓕ Hold down the (SHIFT) key, then drag to create a vertical line perpendicular to the other two lines.

2. Follow these steps to draw a rectangle for the community center and fill it with color:

Ⓐ Select the Rectangle tool.

Ⓑ Make sure the top fill option is selected here.

Ⓒ Position the mouse pointer here, then drag down and to the right to create a rectangle (you do not need to hold down the (SHIFT) key).

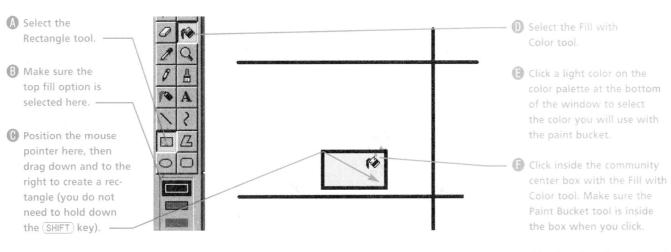

Ⓓ Select the Fill with Color tool.

Ⓔ Click a light color on the color palette at the bottom of the window to select the color you will use with the paint bucket.

Ⓕ Click inside the community center box with the Fill with Color tool. Make sure the Paint Bucket tool is inside the box when you click.

(Continued on the next page)

3. Follow these steps to add a park to the drawing:

TIP!

If you do not like the results of a command, choose Edit→Undo from the menu bar.

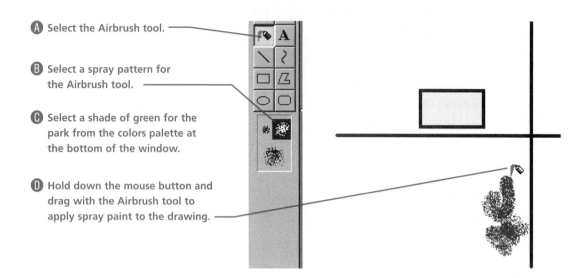

Ⓐ Select the Airbrush tool.

Ⓑ Select a spray pattern for the Airbrush tool.

Ⓒ Select a shade of green for the park from the colors palette at the bottom of the window.

Ⓓ Hold down the mouse button and drag with the Airbrush tool to apply spray paint to the drawing.

Anytime you have completed a substantial amount of work on a project, it is a good idea to save your work. That way if the computer crashes (stops running) or some other problem occurs, you can still open the most recently saved version of the drawing.

4. Choose File→Save from the menu bar to save your drawing.
You will see the floppy drive light go on as the file is saved. Since you have saved this drawing once already (when you set the drawing type), the Save As dialog box does not appear. The blank version of the drawing is replaced by what is on your screen. The drawing is saved with the same settings you made originally.

5. Follow these steps to add a street name to the drawing:

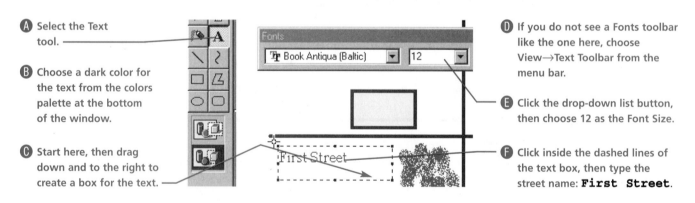

Ⓐ Select the Text tool.

Ⓑ Choose a dark color for the text from the colors palette at the bottom of the window.

Ⓒ Start here, then drag down and to the right to create a box for the text.

Ⓓ If you do not see a Fonts toolbar like the one here, choose View→Text Toolbar from the menu bar.

Ⓔ Click the drop-down list button, then choose 12 as the Font Size.

Ⓕ Click inside the dashed lines of the text box, then type the street name: **First Street**.

6. Add additional street names and the community center name to the drawing as shown below. Don't worry if these are not placed perfectly.

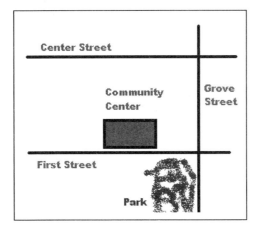

TIP!

If you need to move the Fonts toolbar out of the way, drag on the title bar (where the word Fonts appears on the toolbar).

Paint has many more features than can be covered in this brief tutorial. Most Windows drawing programs use toolboxes and drawing tools that are similar to the Paint tools you have used in this exercise.

Printing Files

Almost all Windows programs have a File→Print command or a Print ⎙ button on a toolbar that you can use to print your documents. The File→Print command usually displays a dialog box that lets you choose the printer, as well as other options. A document with color (such as a Paint drawing) will only print in color if you have a color printer (such as an ink-jet printer). Otherwise, the colors will print as shades of gray.

 ## Hands-On 2.16 **Print the Map**

In this exercise, you will print the drawing you completed in the last exercise..

TIP!

It is always a good idea to save your work before you print.

1. Choose File→Save to save your drawing.

2. Choose File→Print to view the Print dialog box.
   Look over the Print dialog box options for a moment. There is no need to change any of the options.

3. Click OK to print the drawing; retrieve the drawing from the printer.

4. Feel free to enhance your drawing and experiment with some of the other Paint tools.

5. When you are finished with the drawing, choose File→Save from the menu bar to save the finished version of your drawing.

6. Click the Close ☒ button to exit the Paint program. Click Yes if you are asked if you wish to save your drawing.
   If any changes were made since you last gave the Save command, Paint will ask if you wish to save those changes. If you want to discard the most recent changes, you can click No, and the changes will not be saved. Usually, however, you will want to save any changes to a file when you exit a program.

Shutting Down Windows

You must shut down Windows before switching off the computer. The Shut Down command closes all running programs. It also initiates "housekeeping" chores that let Windows start properly the next time the computer is switched on. After the Shut Down command is completed, Windows will display a message indicating that it is safe to switch off power to the computer. On many new computers, the power is switched off automatically.

Logging Off

If you want to leave the computer on for the next user to log on, you should log off Windows rather than shut down the computer. Logging off prevents unauthorized users from accessing network resources. However, if the computer is running Windows 95, 98, or ME, anyone can get to the Windows Desktop by clicking the Cancel button.

Hibernation

Windows 2000, ME, and XP support a feature called Hibernation. Normally, when you shut down the computer all program windows are closed. Hibernation allows you to suspend the computer with program windows open and ready to work again. Windows prepares the computer for hibernation by writing all of the data in RAM onto the hard drive. When you restart the computer, this data is restored to RAM and all program windows and open files appear just as they were when you sent the computer into hibernation. This makes it easy to resume your work.

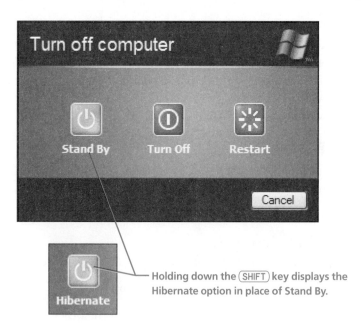

Holding down the (SHIFT) key displays the Hibernate option in place of Stand By.

QUICK REFERENCE: SHUTTING DOWN WINDOWS

Task	Procedure
Log off Windows 98 and ME	■ Click Start on the Windows Taskbar. ■ Choose Log Off [Your User Name] from the Start menu, then click Yes when you are prompted to confirm logging off.
Log off Windows NT 4.0	■ Click Start on the Windows Taskbar, then choose Shut down. ■ Choose the Close all programs and log on as a different user? option and click Yes.
Log off Windows 2000 Professional	■ Click Start on the Windows Taskbar, then choose Shut down. ■ Choose Log Off [Your User Name] from drop-down list and click OK.
Log Off Windows XP	■ Click Start→Log Off. ■ Click Log Off to confirm logging off.
Shut down Windows (all versions except XP)	■ Click Start on the Windows Taskbar, then choose Shut Down. ■ Choose the Shut down option and click Yes or OK.
Shut down Windows (Windows XP only)	■ Click Start. ■ Click Turn Off Computer. ■ Choose the desired shut down method.

 Hands-On 2.17 Log Off Windows

In this exercise, you will log off and leave the computer running for the next user. Your instructor will tell you whether you should log off or shut down the computer at the end of each class session.

1. Click Start, then examine the lower-left side of the Start menu to see which version of Windows you are using.

2. Follow the log-off procedure for the version of windows you are running:

   ■ **Windows 98 and ME**—Click Log Off [Your Log on Name] (just above the Shut Down menu item), then click Yes to confirm logging off.

   ■ **Windows NT**—Click Shut Down, then choose the Close All Programs And Log On As A Different User? option in the dialog box and click Yes.

   ■ **Windows 2000**—Click Shut Down, then choose the Log Off [Your Log on Name] option from the drop-down list and click OK.

   ■ **Windows XP**—Click Start, then click [Log Off] at the bottom of the Start menu, then click the Log Off button.

You should now be logged off, and a sign-on screen should appear.

Concepts Review

True/False Questions

1. Windows is responsible for file, memory, and program management. TRUE FALSE

2. You double-click by pressing the secondary (right) mouse button twice in rapid succession. TRUE FALSE

3. You can start a program by clicking the Start button and choosing the desired program from the Programs menu. TRUE FALSE

4. You use the File→Open command to save a document to a floppy disk. TRUE FALSE

5. Filenames can have up to 255 characters in Windows. TRUE FALSE

6. Windows is a multitasking operating system. TRUE FALSE

7. You can choose as many radio buttons as desired when setting options in a dialog box. TRUE FALSE

8. You should always shut down Windows prior to switching off the computer system. TRUE FALSE

9. The Windows Taskbar lets you switch between program windows. TRUE FALSE

10. You can change the size of a maximized program window by dragging on the window borders. TRUE FALSE

Multiple-Choice Questions

1. Which of the following buttons restores a window?
   a. ▭
   b. ▢
   c. ▤
   d. ☒

2. Which of the following buttons minimizes a window?
   a. ▭
   b. ▢
   c. ▤
   d. ☒

3. Which of the following techniques is used to move a program window?
   a. Maximize the window and drag the Title bar.
   b. Restore the window and drag the Title bar.
   c. Minimize the window and drag the Title bar.
   d. Drag a corner-sizing handle.

4. Which of the following commands can be used to print in most programs?
   a. File→Save
   b. File→Open
   c. View→Print
   d. None of the above

Skill Builders

Skill Builder 2.1 **Type a To Do List**

1. Log on to Windows.

2. Choose Start→Programs→Accessories→WordPad to start the WordPad program. Or use Start→All Programs→Accessories→WordPad if you are running Windows XP.

3. Maximize ▣ the WordPad window.

4. Type **To Do List** as a heading for the document, then tap the (ENTER) key three times to add lines beneath the heading.

5. Type a list of things you need to do this week. Tap (ENTER) twice after each line to double-space the list.

6. Save your list to your exercise diskette using a descriptive name. Make sure that the 3½ Floppy (A:) drive is displayed in the Save in box. Keep in mind that you can use up to 255 characters in the filename including spaces.

7. Use File→Print to print your To Do list.

8. Close ✖ WordPad and save any changes (if WordPad gives you that option).

Skill Builder 2.2 **Paint a House**

1. Start the Paint program with Start→Program→Accessories→Paint. Or use Start→All Programs→Accessories→WordPad if you are running Windows XP.

2. Choose File→Save from the menu bar.

3. Set the Save As Type (at the bottom of the dialog box) to 16 Color Bitmap.
   This setting reduces the number of colors you can use in the drawing, but will significantly reduce the size of the file when you save it.

4. Save the empty drawing to your exercise diskette as **A House**. Make sure that the 3½ Floppy (A:) drive is displayed in the Save in box before you click the Save button.

5. Use your investigative skills, creativity, and some trial and error to draw a house. Try to include objects such as doors, windows, a roof, and perhaps landscaping.

    If you make a mistake, immediately select Edit→Undo from the menu bar to undo your most recent command. If you are running Windows 98 or later, Paint will let you undo the three most recent commands.

6. Feel free to print your drawing.

7. Close Paint, and save any changes (if Paint gives you that option).

Skill Builder 2.3 **Use the Calculator**

This Skill Builder will show you how to use the Windows Calculator applet.

1. Click the Start [Start] button and slide the mouse up to Programs (or All Programs if you are running Windows XP).

2. Slide the mouse to Accessories and choose Calculator. If you are running Windows 2000, ME, or XP and you do not see the Calculator in the Accessories menu, click the Menu Extension [⟨⟨] command in the list to display the entire Accessories menu.

3. Follow these steps to add two numbers:

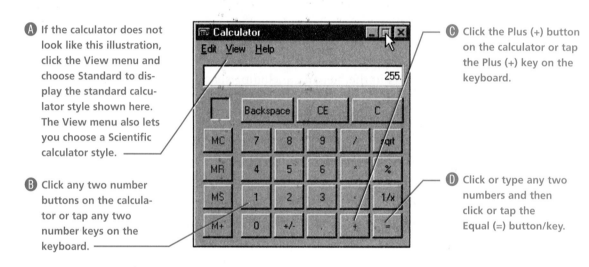

Ⓐ If the calculator does not look like this illustration, click the View menu and choose Standard to display the standard calculator style shown here. The View menu also lets you choose a Scientific calculator style.

Ⓑ Click any two number buttons on the calculator or tap any two number keys on the keyboard.

Ⓒ Click the Plus (+) button on the calculator or tap the Plus (+) key on the keyboard.

Ⓓ Click or type any two numbers and then click or tap the Equal (=) button/key.

4. Feel free to experiment with the calculator.

5. Click the Minimize [_] button to minimize the calculator.

6. Click the Calculator [Calculator] button on the Taskbar to restore the calculator. *Notice that you can hide the calculator when you are not using it and display it when you need it. This technique is often used when working with multiple programs.*

7. Close [X] the calculator window when you have finished experimenting, then continue with the Assessment exercises.

Assessments

Assessment 2.1 Create and Save a WordPad Document

1. Start the WordPad program.

2. Type the document displayed below.

   Your document does not have to match this document exactly, but it should contain the same information.

Parts of a Personal Computer System

Hardware
System Unit
Monitor
Mouse
Keyboard
Printer

Software
Operating System
Application Programs
User Files

[Your Name]

---

3. Save the document to your exercise diskette as **Assessment Exercise for Lesson 2**.

4. Close ☒ the document.

Assessment 2.2 **Open and Print a WordPad Document**

1. Start the WordPad Program.

2. Open the Assessment Exercise For Lesson 2 document you created in the previous assessment exercise.

3. Change the title of the document to **Personal Computer Components**.

4. Save the change to the document, then print the document. Retrieve the printout from the printer.

5. Close WordPad.

6. Turn in the printed page for grading.

Assessment 2.3 **Configure Two Program Windows**

1. Start the WordPad Program.

2. If WordPad is maximized, click the Restore button to restore the window.

3. Drag on WordPad's program window borders so that the WordPad window covers the left half of the Desktop.

4. Start the Paint Program. Make sure the Paint window is not maximized.

5. Drag on Paint's program window borders so that the Paint window covers the right half of the Desktop.

6. Have your instructor or a lab assistant initial that you have completed this assessment exercise successfully. _____

7. Close the program windows.

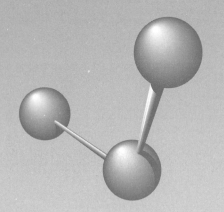

LESSON 3

File Management and Online Help

When you begin working with a computer, you will have just a few files to keep track of. But as your use of the computer grows, so will the number of files you must manage. After several months, you can have over a hundred of your own files. After a year, you can have hundreds more. Fortunately, Windows gives you a very effective tool for managing files: folders. With folders, you can group related files together. You can even create folders inside of other folders. As you learn how to use new features such as folders, you should take advantage of the excellent online Help system featured in Windows. Online Help makes it easy to find the answer to many types of questions with three ways to search for the information you need.

See the Lesson 3 Web Page at: labpub.com/learn/bc/ccw/lesson3

Case Study

Chantal is taking four courses at her community college. As she goes over the syllabi, Chantal notices that three of her courses will require her to submit term papers. She decides to prepare for some of the research she must do. Chantal creates several folders on her computer to help her organize the files she will accumulate as she performs research for each term paper. She creates a folder for each of her classes on the computer. Then she creates folders inside the class folders to further organize her files. For example, she creates Final and Drafts folders for the word processor documents she will create. Chantal also creates a Research folder to hold the various files, Web pages, and notes she will collect. She creates a folder called Old Stuff for everything she thinks she doesn't need, but does not want to delete. She can delete the Old Stuff folder after the term project paper is completed.

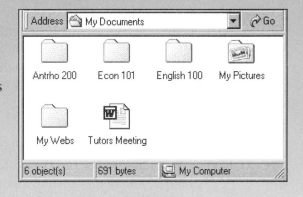

Chantal created these folders inside each of her course folders. This makes it easier for her to find the files she needs to work on as the semester progresses.

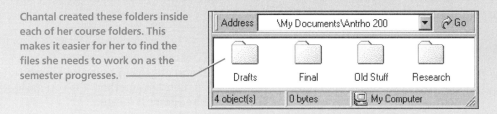

As Chantal learns new ways to organize her work, she also learns how to look up the answers to her questions with online Help. For example, when she could not recall how to create a new folder on her computer, she looked it up in online Help. Chantal likes to be as self-reliant as possible where computers are concerned, and online Help is one of the ways she can do this.

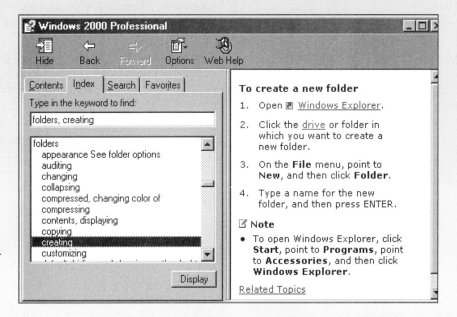

Using Online Help with Windows

Windows provides an online Help system that can answer questions about running application programs or completing tasks with Windows itself. Online Help has proven so effective that many vendors no longer publish the sort of lengthy manuals that used to come with most programs. For example, the Microsoft Office XP Suite provides just a thin "Discovering" manual with an overview of what's new and how to use basic features of the software.

Finding the Information You Need

Your goal when using online Help is to locate a Help topic. The Help feature provides several methods that you can use to locate topics. All Help topics have keywords that identify them. For example, a Help topic that discusses copying files can probably be located by using the keywords *copying files*. Regardless of which method you use, the goal is to locate a topic. Once you locate the desired topic, you can display it and follow its instructions.

Search Methods

Depending on the version of Windows you are using, the following methods are available for searching online Help:

Search Method	Description
Contents	The Contents method is useful if you are trying to locate a topic but you aren't really sure how to describe it. The Contents method lets you navigate through a series of categories until the desired topic is located.
Index	The Index method lets you locate a topic by typing keywords. An alphabetically indexed list of topics is displayed from which you can choose the desired topic. This method is most useful if you know the name of the topic or feature with which you need assistance.
Search (Called Find in Windows NT)	The Search method searches inside of the Help topics for the keywords you enter. This provides an in-depth search and lets you locate topics that may not be found using the other search methods. However, sometimes this method will find more topics than you need.
Web Help (Windows 98, ME, and 2000 only)	This Help option takes you directly to Microsoft's Web site. Web Help can locate the latest information on the topic for which you are searching.

QUICK REFERENCE: STARTING ONLINE HELP

Task	Procedure
Start Windows online Help.	■ Choose Start→Help from the Start menu. ■ Choose the desired search method.
Start online Help in an application program.	■ Choose Help from the menu bar or tap the (F1) function key, then select the type of Help you require.

Hands-On 3.1 Search Online Help

In the first step of this exercise, you will determine which version of Windows you are running. This will determine whether you perform section a, b, or c of the exercise.

1. Click the Start button. Read the version of Windows you are running in the vertical title that appears along the left side of the Start menu. Click the Start button again to close the menu.

2. Select the Hands-On exercise for the version of Windows you are running.

   - **Windows 98**—Complete Hands-On Exercise 3.1a immediately below.

   - **Windows NT**—Complete Hands-On Exercise 3.1b on page 82.

   - **Windows 2000**—Complete Hands-On Exercise 3.1c on page 83.

   - **Windows ME**—Complete Hands-on Exercise 3.1d on page 84.

   - **Windows XP**—Complete Hands-on Exercise 3.1e on page 85.

Hands-On 3.1a Search Online Help in Windows 98

Windows 98 introduced a new way to search online Help. It is based on navigation techniques used with Web browsers. In Windows 98, you open Help categories with a single click.

1. Click the Start button and choose ![Help] from the menu.
   The Windows Help window will appear. In the next few steps, you will look up a Help topic on copying files or folders.

2. Follow these steps to conduct a search using the Contents method:

Ⓐ Make sure the Contents tab is selected. Most of the items in this list are "books" that represent the various categories of Help information available.

Ⓑ Click to open the Exploring Your Computer category. Notice how this book "opens" to reveal additional categories.

Ⓒ Click to open the Files and Folders category.

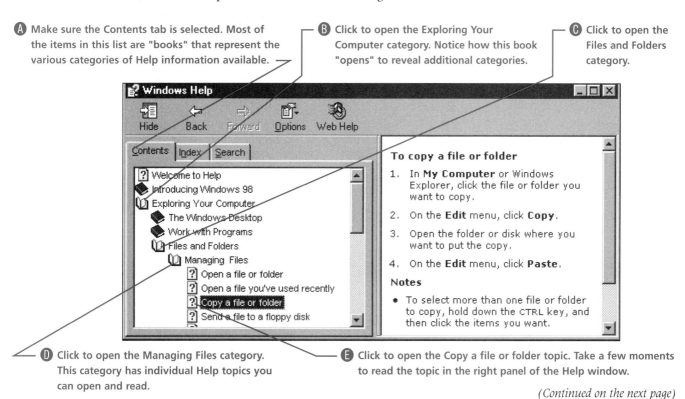

Ⓓ Click to open the Managing Files category. This category has individual Help topics you can open and read.

Ⓔ Click to open the Copy a file or folder topic. Take a few moments to read the topic in the right panel of the Help window.

(Continued on the next page)

3. Follow these steps to adjust the size of the panels in the Help window:

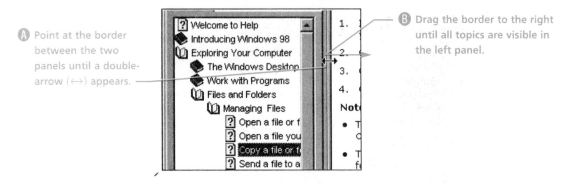

Ⓐ Point at the border between the two panels until a double-arrow (↔) appears.

Ⓑ Drag the border to the right until all topics are visible in the left panel.

4. Click the Hide button on the left side of the Help window toolbar.
This command conserves screen space by hiding the category list. Now only the Help topic you displayed earlier is visible.

5. Click the Show button on the left side of the Help window toolbar.
Now the category list is visible again; thus, this control works as a toggle to switch the display of the category list on and off.

Leave the Help window open, and continue with the Index Search topic on page 86.

 Hands-On 3.1b Search Online Help in Windows NT

1. Click the Start button and choose [Help] from the menu.
The Windows Help window will appear. In the next few steps, you will look up a Help topic on copying files or folders.

2. Follow these steps to conduct a search using the Contents method:

Ⓐ Make sure the Contents tab is selected. Most of the items in this list are "books" that represent the various categories of Help information available.

Ⓑ Double-click to open the How To category. Notice how this book "opens" to reveal additional categories.

Ⓒ Double-click to open the Work with Files and Folders category. This category has individual Help topics you can open and read.

Ⓓ Double-click to open the Copying a file or folder topic. Notice that the Help Topics window disappears, and a new Topic window appears.

Ⓔ Take a few moments to read the Help topic. When you are finished, click the Help Topics button near the top-left corner of the Topic window. This will display the Help Topics window once again.

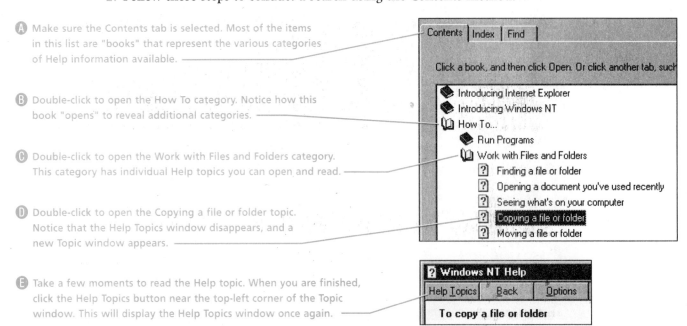

Leave the Help window open, and continue with the Index Search topic on page 86.

1. Click the Start button, and choose ![Help] from the menu.
   The Windows Help window will appear. In the next few steps, you will look up a Help topic on copying files or folders.

2. Follow these steps to conduct a search using the Contents method:

Ⓐ Make sure the Contents tab is selected. Most of the items in this list are "books" that represent the various categories of Help information available.

Ⓑ Click to open the Files and Folders category.

Ⓒ Click to open the Copy or move a file or folder topic. Take a few moments to read the topic in the right panel of the Help window.

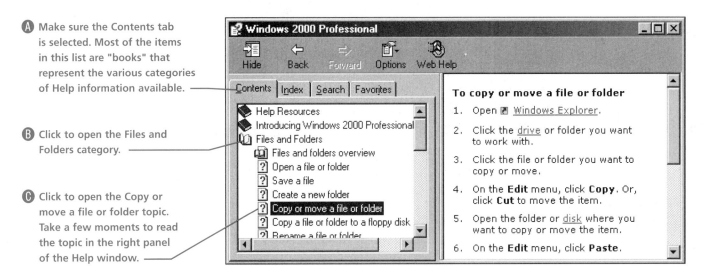

3. Follow these steps to adjust the size of the panels in the Help window:

Ⓐ Point at the border between the two panels until you see a double-arrow (↔) appear.

Ⓑ Drag the border to the right until all topics are visible in the left panel.

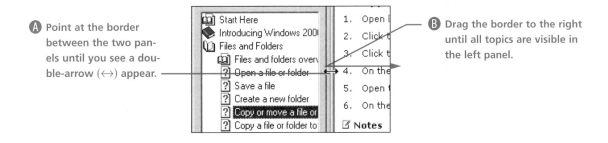

4. Click the Hide button on the left side of the Help window toolbar.
   This command conserves screen space by hiding the category list. Now only the Help topic you displayed earlier is visible.

5. Click the Show button on the left side of the Help window toolbar.
   Now the category list is visible again; thus, this control works as a toggle to switch the display of the category list on and off.

   Leave the Help window open, and continue with the Index Search topic on page 86.

Hands-On 3.1d Search Online Help in Windows ME

Windows ME introduced an improved Help system. It contains a table of contents navigation scheme that is easier to use. It also features tours and direct links to Web pages.

1. Click the Start button and choose ⬡ Help from the menu.
   The Windows Help window will appear. In the next few steps, you will look up a Help topic on copying files or folders.

2. Click the Programs, Files, & Folders link.

A new sub-list of Help topics appears.

3. Click the Managing Files & Folders link (third from the bottom).
4. Click the Copying or moving files or folders topic.

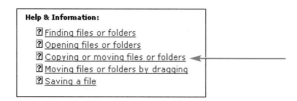

Now the detailed Help instructions appear in the right panel of the Help window.

5. Follow these steps to adjust the size of the panels in the Help window:

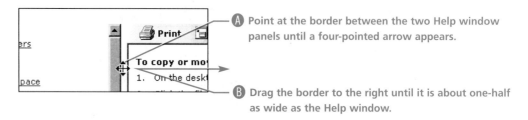

Depending on the screen size of your monitor, you may sometimes wish to change the area displaying Help instructions.

6. Point at the border between the Help panels and drag the border to the left until the left panel is about one-quarter as wide as the Help window.
   Leave the Help window open and continue with the Index Search topic on page 86.

Hands-On 3.1e Search Online Help in Windows XP

Windows XP continues the refinements in the Windows Help system introduced in Windows ME. It contains a table of contents navigation scheme that is easier to use.

1. Click the Start button and choose Help and Support 🔵 Help and Support from the menu.
   The Windows Help window will appear. In the next few steps, you will look up a Help topic on copying files or folders.

2. Click the Windows Basics link.

The Windows Basics topic list appears.

3. Follow these steps to display details on copying files:

Ⓐ Click the plus sign beside Core Windows tasks. This expands a list of subtopics.

Ⓑ Click Working with files and folders. A further list of topics appears in the right panel of the Help window.

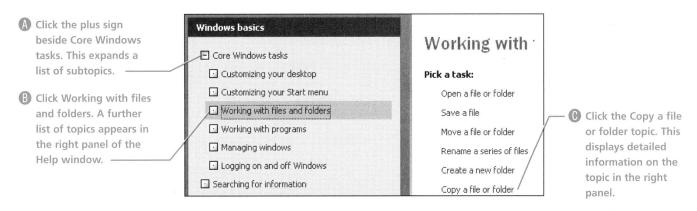

Ⓒ Click the Copy a file or folder topic. This displays detailed information on the topic in the right panel.

4. Follow these steps to adjust the size of the panels in the Help window:

Ⓐ Point at the border between the two Help window panels until a double-pointed arrow appears.

Ⓑ Drag the border to the right until it is about one-half as wide as the Help window.

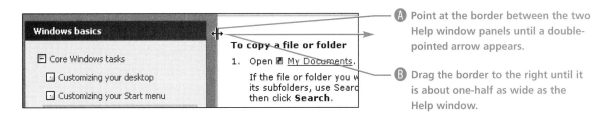

Depending on the screen size of your monitor, you may sometimes wish to change the area displaying Help instructions.

5. Point at the border between the Help panels and drag the border to the left until the left panel is a good size to display the Windows Basics topics.
   Leave the Help window open and continue with the Index Search topic on page 86.

Index Search

The Index search lets you find Help topics by searching for a keyword in the topic titles. Every topic that includes the keyword in its title is displayed in a search results window.

 ## Hands-On 3.2 **Search with the Index Method**

In this exercise, you will use the Index search method to find the same topic on copying files and folders.

1. Follow the steps for your version of Windows to perform an Index search:

Windows 98, NT, 2000

Ⓐ Click the Index tab near the top of the Help window.

Ⓑ Type the keyword **copying** in the keyword box.

Ⓒ Look over the search results in this list, then use the instructions in the next step to open the appropriate topic.

Ⓓ Go on to Step 2 on page 87.

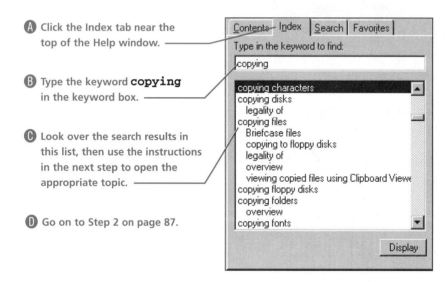

Windows ME

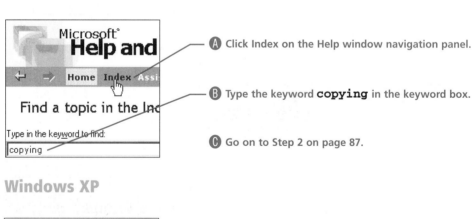

Ⓐ Click Index on the Help window navigation panel.

Ⓑ Type the keyword **copying** in the keyword box.

Ⓒ Go on to Step 2 on page 87.

Windows XP

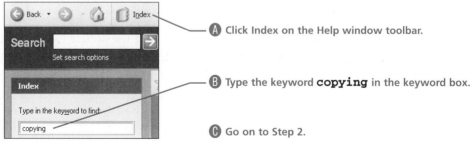

Ⓐ Click Index on the Help window toolbar.

Ⓑ Type the keyword **copying** in the keyword box.

Ⓒ Go on to Step 2.

2. Follow the instructions for the version of Windows you are using:

Note: Instructions for Windows, ME, and XP are on the following page.

Windows 98

Ⓐ Double-click the overview topic under copying files, folders. The topic will be displayed in the right panel of the Help window.

Ⓑ Go on to Step 3 on page 88.

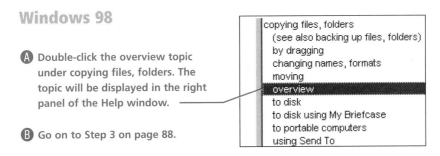

Windows NT 4.0

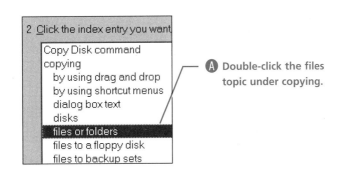

Ⓐ Double-click the files topic under copying.

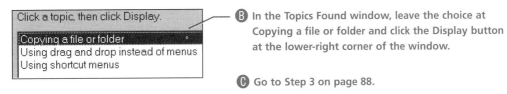

Ⓑ In the Topics Found window, leave the choice at Copying a file or folder and click the Display button at the lower-right corner of the window.

Ⓒ Go to Step 3 on page 88.

Windows 2000

Ⓐ Double-click the overview topic under copying files.

Ⓑ Choose Copy or move a file or folder from the Topics Found window, then click the Display button at the lower-right corner of the window. The topic will be displayed in the right panel of the Help window.

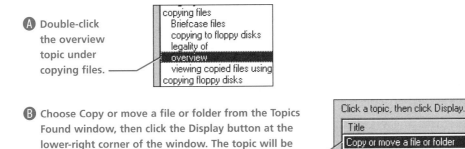

Ⓒ Go to Step 3 on page 88.

(Continued on the next page)

2. Follow the instruction for the version of Windows you are using (continued).

Windows ME

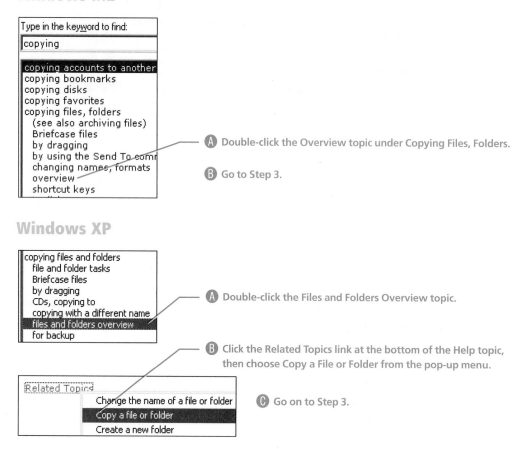

Type in the keyword to find:

copying

copying accounts to another
copying bookmarks
copying disks
copying favorites
copying files, folders
  (see also archiving files)
  Briefcase files
  by dragging
  by using the Send To comr
  changing names, formats
  overview
  shortcut keys

Ⓐ Double-click the Overview topic under Copying Files, Folders.

Ⓑ Go to Step 3.

Windows XP

copying files and folders
  file and folder tasks
  Briefcase files
  by dragging
  CDs, copying to
  copying with a different name
  files and folders overview
  for backup

Ⓐ Double-click the Files and Folders Overview topic.

Ⓑ Click the Related Topics link at the bottom of the Help topic, then choose Copy a File or Folder from the pop-up menu.

Related Topics
  Change the name of a file or folder
  Copy a file or folder
  Create a new folder

Ⓒ Go on to Step 3.

3. Follow the steps for your version of Windows to return to the Contents search method:

   ▪ **Windows 98, NT, 2000**—Click the Contents tab.

   ▪ **Windows ME**—Click Home near the top of the window. ⟵ ⟶ Home

   ▪ **Windows XP**—Click the Home ⌂ button on the Toolbar.

4. Use the Contents search method to browse for new features in your version of Windows. Look for topics such as Introducing Windows, or Using Windows, What's New....

5. Use the Index search method to search for help on the following topics.

   ▪ Cascading Windows

   ▪ Undeleting Files

6. When you are finished with the additional searches in Step 5, close ☒ any open Help windows before moving on to the next topic.

Accessing Help in an Application Program

FROM THE KEYBOARD

(F1) to display the Help system.

Most Windows programs have online Help built into them. You access a program's online Help system with the Help command from the program's menu bar. Many Windows application programs use an online Help window that works just like Windows Help. The Microsoft XP Office Suite features a question box and an Office Assistant that allows you to search for Help topics by typing a question in plain English.

Office Assistants let you search for help with simple questions.

 ## Hands-On 3.3 Look Up Help for an Application Program

In this exercise, you will start the WordPad program and look up a Help topic in WordPad's online Help.

1. Choose Start→Programs→Accessories→WordPad to start the WordPad program.

2. Choose Help→Help Topics from WordPad's menu bar.
   WordPad displays its Help window. Unless you are running Windows ME, this window will look similar to the Help window you used in the previous exercises.

3. Choose the Index tab, then type **undo** as the search keyword.
   A list of Help topics beginning with the same letters as this keyword will appear.

4. Double-click to open the topic in the results list that begins with the word undo or undoing.
   WordPad's Help displays a method to undo your most recent action. This can be useful if you accidentally delete some text or make some other mistake as you work.

5. Click the Help Window's Close ☒ button.

6. Tap the (F1) function key in the top row of keys on the keyboard.
   Most Windows programs treat (F1) as the Help key.

7. Close ☒ the Help window again.

8. Close ☒ the WordPad window.

Browsing through Files

In Lesson 2, you stored documents and an image as files on your exercise diskette. In this lesson, you will learn how to organize the growing number of files that can accumulate as you work with a computer. Besides your own files, there are hundreds or even thousands of files on the hard drive that run Windows and the application programs you use. Learning how all these files are organized will help you save and find your own files more easily.

How Files are Organized

Windows uses a flexible hierarchy that is common to most personal computers. The three levels in the hierarchy are listed below:

Level	Definition	Examples
Drive	This is a physical place in which you store files.	■ A floppy disk ■ A hard drive
Folder	This is an electronic location in which you store groups of related files. It is also possible to place folders inside of other folders.	■ A folder to store all the files for an application program ■ A folder to store all the letters you type for a project
File	This is a collection of computer data that has some common purpose.	■ A letter you've typed ■ A picture you've drawn

Browsing with the My Computer Window

As you work with Windows programs such as WordPad and Paint, you will want to locate **My Computer** and open files you have created previously. Although you can open files from within an application program, sometimes it is more convenient to search directly through all of the files you have saved to a hard drive or floppy disk. This is the sort of task for which the My Computer window is perfectly suited.

The following illustrations describe the major features of the My Computer window. Take a moment to review these features before beginning the next Hands-On exercise.

Windows 98

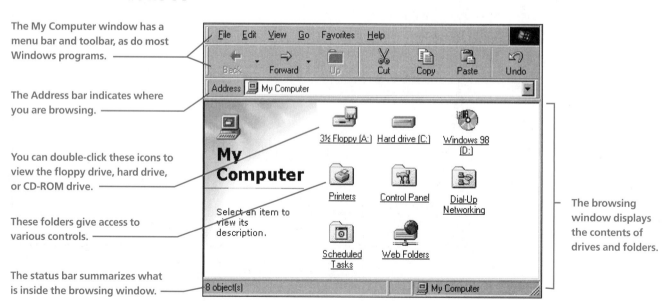

The My Computer window has a menu bar and toolbar, as do most Windows programs.

The Address bar indicates where you are browsing.

You can double-click these icons to view the floppy drive, hard drive, or CD-ROM drive.

These folders give access to various controls.

The status bar summarizes what is inside the browsing window.

The browsing window displays the contents of drives and folders.

Windows 2000 and ME

The toolbar in Windows 2000/ME differs slightly from earlier versions of Windows.

This button displays the drives and folders on the system in a new panel.

These buttons let you move, copy, and delete files.

These links display other useful locations in which files and folders may be stored.

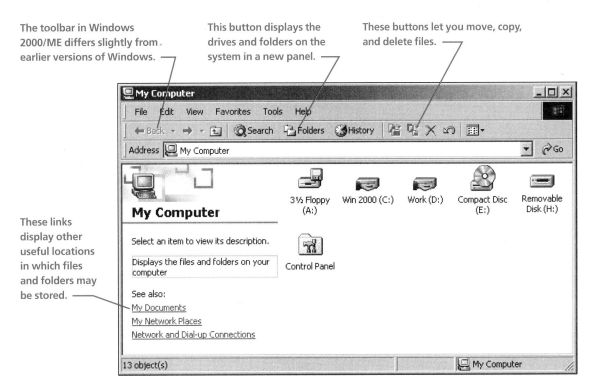

Windows XP

You can double-click any items in this panel to view their contents.

The address bar displays the location you are currently browsing.

These panels contain links to display system task commands and other places you may wish to browse.

This panel displays details on whichever item you select in the right panel.

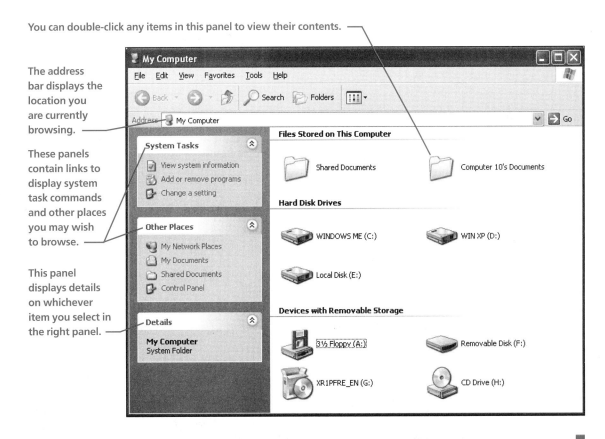

Hands-On 3.4 Open a My Computer Window

In this exercise, you will open a My Computer window and view the contents of your exercise diskette.

1. Close ☒ any open windows on the Desktop.

2. Double-click the My Computer ▣ icon near the top-left corner of the Desktop, or click Start→My Computer if you are running Windows XP.

3. If the My Computer window is not already maximized, maximize ▣ the window now.

4. Choose View→Large Icons (or Icons in Windows XP) from the menu bar.
   This view may have already been selected. It displays easy-to-recognize icons for all of the drives, folders, and files on the computer. Notice the icons for the floppy drive, hard drive, and CD-ROM drive.

5. Follow the instructions below for your version of windows:

Windows 98

- Choose View→Folder Options from the menu bar.

- Click the Custom option.

  ⊙ C̲ustom, based on settings you choose:

- Click the Settings button.

- Make sure that the Browse folders as follows option is set to "Same Window," as shown at right.

  ┌─ Browse folders as follows ─────────┐
  │ ⊙ Open each folder in the sa̲me window │
  │ ○ Open each folder in its own w̲indow │
  └──────────────────────────────────┘

- Click OK, then click the Close button to close the dialog box.

Windows NT

- Click View on the menu bar. Follow the instructions in the Windows 98 section above if the last item in the view menu reads Folder Options. Otherwise, click Options in the View menu.

  ┌──────────────────────────────────────┐
  │ ⊙ Browse folders by using a si̲ngle window that changes │
  │   as you open each folder.   │
  │   │
  │   Example: ┌────────┐   │
  │   │░░░░░░░░│   │
  │   └────────┘   │
  └──────────────────────────────────────┘

- Make sure that the Folders option is set to "Single Window," as shown at right.

- Click OK to close the dialog box.

Windows 2000, ME, and XP

- Choose Tools→Folder Options from the menu bar.

- Make sure that the Browse Folders option is set to "Same Window," as shown at right.

  ┌─ Browse Folders ─────────────────────┐
  │ ▣▬▬ ⊙ Open each folder in the same window │
  │ ▤▤   ○ Open each folder in its own window │
  └──────────────────────────────────────┘

- Click OK to close the dialog box.

6. Place your exercise diskette in the floppy drive, with the label side up and the metal side in.

7. Double-click the 3½ Floppy (A:) ▤ or ▣ icon to view the exercise diskette.
   You stored some files on this diskette in the previous lesson. But WordPad's Open and Save As dialog boxes only display document files that the program can open. In the My Computer window you can see all of the files on the diskette. Leave the My Computer window open and continue with the next topic.

Opening Files

When you double-click on a file in a My Computer window, the program used to create or edit that type of file is launched and the file is displayed in the program window. This is a convenient way to start working with a file after you find it.

 Hands-On 3.5 Open a Document File

In this exercise, you will open the WordPad document you created in a previous lesson.

1. Double-click on the Tutor Meeting document file.
   Windows will start the program that is associated with document files. This will probably be Microsoft Word or WordPad. If Word is installed on the computer, it is programmed to open files that were created with WordPad. However, you can also start WordPad from the Start menu and use WordPad's Open command to open the file.

2. Click the upper Close ☒ button, as shown at right. Click No if you are asked to save the file.
   Now only the My Computer window should be open.

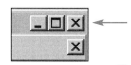

Changing the View

There are several ways to view drives and folders in a My Computer window. You have been using the Large Icons view thus far. This view represents each file and folder with a larger icon than the other views. You can change the view from the My Computer View menu or with the Views toolbar button. Depending on the version of Windows you are using, the Views button(s) will match one of the examples below:

Windows 98 and NT   **Windows 2000**   **Windows ME**   **Windows XP**   The view buttons on some Windows 95 and NT Toolbars may look like this.

Hands-On 3.6 **Try out Different Views**

In this exercise, you will experiment with different formats for viewing files.

1. Choose View→List from the menu bar.
   Use this view when you want to display as many folder and file names as possible.

2. Choose View→Details from the menu bar.
   This view gives you additional information about the files, such as the date each file was created or modified. Depending on how this view was last used, you may or may not be able to see the entire filename in the leftmost column.

3. Follow these steps to adjust the width of a column in Details view:

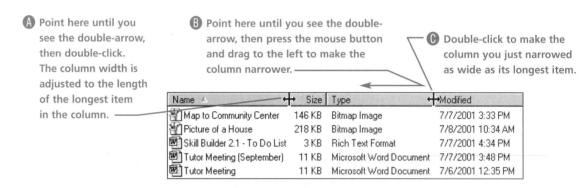

Ⓐ Point here until you see the double-arrow, then double-click. The column width is adjusted to the length of the longest item in the column.

Ⓑ Point here until you see the double-arrow, then press the mouse button and drag to the left to make the column narrower.

Ⓒ Double-click to make the column you just narrowed as wide as its longest item.

Name △	Size	Type	Modified
Map to Community Center	146 KB	Bitmap Image	7/7/2001 3:33 PM
Picture of a House	218 KB	Bitmap Image	7/8/2001 10:34 AM
Skill Builder 2.1 - To Do List	3 KB	Rich Text Format	7/7/2001 4:34 PM
Tutor Meeting (September)	11 KB	Microsoft Word Document	7/7/2001 3:48 PM
Tutor Meeting	11 KB	Microsoft Word Document	7/6/2001 12:35 PM

4. If you are running Windows 2000, ME, or XP, choose View→Thumbnails from the menu bar. After you have seen the Thumbnails view, return to the Details view.
   The Thumbnails view displays a miniature view of each image file. Notice that the map you created in Lesson 2 is now displayed as a small thumbnail image.

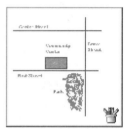

Map to Community Center

Sorting Files

The My Computer window may contain many files and folders. You can sort the files and folders in a variety of ways. This can be useful if you are trying to find a specific file. The files and folders can be sorted by name, size, type, or date. These four parameters are known as Sort Keys. You can also sort files in ascending order (A to Z) or descending order (Z to A). The four sort keys are described in the following table.

Sort Key	How it Sorts the Files and Folders
Name	Alphabetically by filename
Size	By the size of the files
Type	By the function of the file, such as word processing document, spreadsheet, or database
Date	By the date that the file was created or most recently modified

Hands-On 3.7 Sort the Files

In this exercise, you will view the files on your exercise diskette in various sort orders.

1. Make sure that the Details view is displayed, then follow these steps to sort the files in various ways:

Ⓐ Click the Modified or Date Modified column heading to sort the files by date. The most recently modified file is listed first. ——

Ⓑ Click the Modified or Date Modified column heading again. Now files with the most recent date are at the bottom of the list. When you click the same column a second time, the list is sorted in descending rather than ascending order. ——

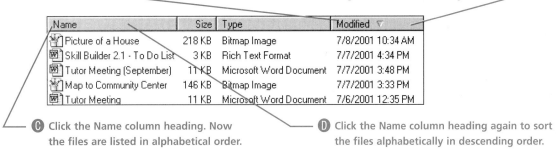

Name	Size	Type	Modified ▽
Picture of a House	218 KB	Bitmap Image	7/8/2001 10:34 AM
Skill Builder 2.1 - To Do List	3 KB	Rich Text Format	7/7/2001 4:34 PM
Tutor Meeting (September)	11 KB	Microsoft Word Document	7/7/2001 3:48 PM
Map to Community Center	146 KB	Bitmap Image	7/7/2001 3:33 PM
Tutor Meeting	11 KB	Microsoft Word Document	7/6/2001 12:35 PM

Ⓒ Click the Name column heading. Now the files are listed in alphabetical order.

Ⓓ Click the Name column heading again to sort the files alphabetically in descending order.

2. Try sorting the files by clicking on the other columns.
   Sorting the files can often help you locate a particular file. For example, sorting the files by date can help you find a file you created or modified recently.

3. Set the view to Large Icons (or Icons).
   You can also sort files when you are in one of the other view modes, as you will do in the next step.

4. Choose View→Arrange Icons→By Size from the menu bar.
   Your Map to Community Center file should be last in the list. Image files like the map are usually much larger than word processing documents. The Tutor Meeting file appears toward the top of the list, because it is a very small document.

5. Close ☒ the My Computer window.

Working with Folders

Folders are important tools for organizing files. You may have just a few files when you begin using a computer, but after a year or two you may have hundreds of files. What if you could only view your files in a single, long list? This would be similar to finding a book in a library that had only one long bookshelf. You could find the book eventually, but you would need to scan through many titles first.

Folders Hierarchy

Folders are organized into a hierarchy on each drive of a Windows system. Windows creates many folders when it is installed on the computer. You can create your own folders as well. The following illustration displays a common folders hierarchy on a Windows system. This is an example of the *Exploring* window. You will learn how to open an Exploring window later in this lesson.

Here is the floppy drive. This floppy disk has two folders on it that were created by a user.

The Documents folder is selected for viewing. Notice how it is "open." The contents of the folder are displayed in the right panel of the Exploring window.

This is the computer's hard drive. It contains several folders that were created when Windows was installed and still more folders that were created as new programs were installed.

The plus signs (+) beside these folders indicate that some folders are not displayed. Clicking the plus sign expands the list to display folders contained within a folder.

This panel displays the contents of any drive or folder that is selected in the left panel.

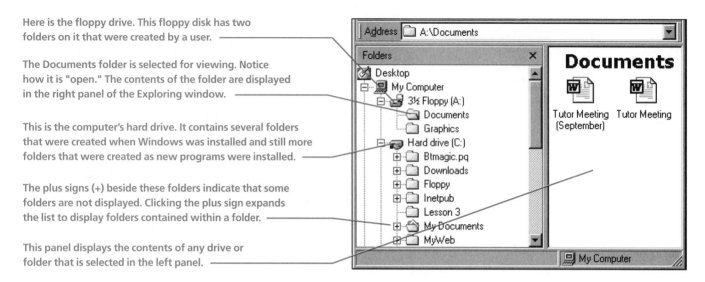

The My Documents Folder

Windows 98, 2000, ME, and XP feature a special folder called My Documents. This folder stores files on the computer's hard drive. The My Documents folder is associated with your log-on name. This means that each user with his or her own log on name has a unique My Documents folder. If you are running a program in the Office XP Suite, you can access the My Documents folder with a single click.

This button in the Word 2002 Save As dialog box navigates you to the My Documents folder with a single click.

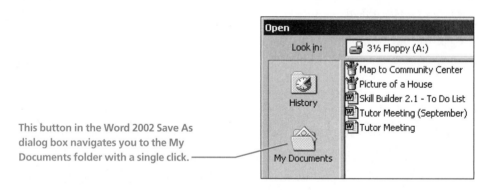

Creating Folders

You can create folders on a floppy disk or the hard drive whenever you need them. Folders can be created while you are viewing a drive in a My Computer or Exploring window. You can also create folders from the Save As dialog box of most Windows programs.

See the Web page for this lesson to view a video on sizing program windows.

QUICK REFERENCE: HOW TO CREATE A FOLDER

Task	Procedure
Create a folder from a My Computer window.	■ Open a My Computer Window. ■ Navigate to the drive or folder in which you wish to create the new folder. ■ Choose File→New→Folder from the menu bar. ■ Type a name for the new folder, then tap the (ENTER) key.
Create a folder in the Save As dialog box of an application program.	■ Choose File→Save As from the program's menu bar. ■ Click the Create New Folder 🗀 button near the top of the Save As window. ■ Type a name for the new folder, then click OK.

Hands-On 3.8 Create Folders on Your Floppy Disk

In this exercise, you will create two folders on your exercise diskette. Later in this lesson you will move and copy files into these folders.

1. Double-click the My Computer 🖳 icon near the top-left corner of the Desktop or click Start→My Computer if you are running Windows XP. If necessary, Maximize 🗖 the window.

2. Make sure your exercise diskette is in the floppy drive.

3. Double-click the 3½ Floppy (A:) 🖴 or 🖴 icon to view the exercise diskette.

4. Make sure the view is set to Large Icons (or Icons in Windows XP).

5. Follow these steps to create a new folder on your floppy disk:

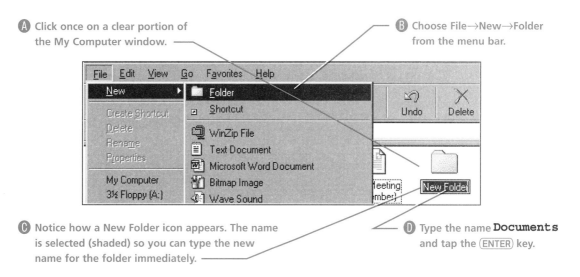

Ⓐ Click once on a clear portion of the My Computer window.

Ⓑ Choose File→New→Folder from the menu bar.

Ⓒ Notice how a New Folder icon appears. The name is selected (shaded) so you can type the new name for the folder immediately.

Ⓓ Type the name **Documents** and tap the (ENTER) key.

(Continued on the next page)

6. Double-click the Documents folder icon to navigate to your new folder.
   Notice that the name of your folder is displayed in the Address bar near the top of the My Computer window as well as in the Title bar. This folder is empty now, but you will place files in it later. If you are running Windows NT, you may not see the word Address next to the Address bar.

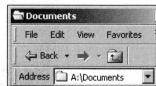

7. Follow these steps to navigate back to the 3½ Floppy (A:) level:

   Ⓐ Click the Address bar drop-down list button. This button will be on the right side of the My Computer window.

   Ⓑ Click this scroll button if you do not see the 3½ Floppy (A:) drive in the drop down list.

   Ⓒ Click 3½ Floppy (A:) in the list.

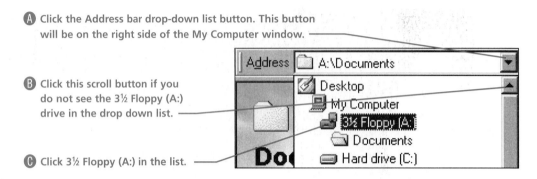

   Now the 3½ Floppy (A:) drive is displayed in the Address bar. Looking at the Address bar as you navigate in folders helps you keep track of where you are.

8. Choose File→New→Folder from the menu bar. Type **Graphics** as the name for the new folder, and tap the (ENTER) key.

9. Double-click on the Graphics folder.
   Notice that the name of the folder is displayed in the Address bar.

10. Click the Up [icon] or [icon] button on the toolbar to return to the 3½ Floppy (A:) drive level.
    The Up button jumps you one level up in the drive/folder hierarchy. This button is often easier to use than the drop-down list you used in Step 7.

Renaming Files and Folders

In Lesson 2, you learned how to save a file with a new name to create a copy of the file. It is also easy to rename a file without making a copy. To rename a file that is displayed in a My Computer window, right-click on the file and choose Rename from the pop-up menu.

QUICK REFERENCE: HOW TO RENAME A FILE OR FOLDER

Task	Procedure
Rename a file or folder with the right-click method.	▪ Right-click on the file or folder icon, then choose Rename from the pop-up menu. ▪ Type the new name, then tap the (ENTER) key.
Rename a file or folder with the click-pause method.	▪ Click on once the filename. ▪ Pause about 2 seconds then click on the filename again. ▪ Type the new name, then tap the (ENTER) key.

Filename Extensions

Most Windows filenames have an extension that consists of three letters following a period at the end of the filename. Filename extensions identify the type of file you are working with. For example, the Tutor Meeting file is a word processing document, so it has a filename extension of .doc. Windows application programs add this extension to any filename you type when you save a file. Most Windows systems hide the filename extension. But if your system is set to display it, you must type out the extension whenever you rename a file.

The filename —————— Tutor Meeting.doc —— The extension. Most Windows systems are set to hide the extension

Hands-On 3.9 Rename a File

In this exercise, you will use both methods to rename one of the files you created in Lesson 2.

1. Follow these steps to issue the Rename command with the right-click method:

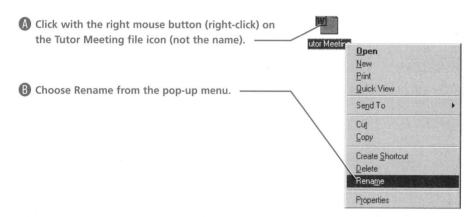

Ⓐ Click with the right mouse button (right-click) on the Tutor Meeting file icon (not the name).

Ⓑ Choose Rename from the pop-up menu.

   Windows highlights the filename for renaming. It may or may not display a three-letter extension of .doc.

2. Examine the filename, then follow the instructions that match the filename:

   ▪ If the filename reads Tutor Meeting, type **April Meeting** and tap (ENTER).

   ▪ If the filename reads Tutor Meeting.doc, type **April Meeting.doc** and tap (ENTER).

   The old name is deleted and replaced by the new name.

3. Click on a clear area of the My Computer window to deselect the April Meeting file.

4. Click on the filename (not the icon) for the April Meeting file. Pause about two seconds, and then click again on the filename.
   The name will be highlighted for editing. You need to pause so that Windows does not mistake your command for a double-click (which is done much faster).

5. Tap the left arrow ⊖ key until the insertion point is blinking just to the right of the *l* in April, then tap the (BACKSPACE) key until the word April is deleted.
   The arrow key allows you to move the insertion point back without deleting the word Meeting.

6. Type **Tutor** as the first word in the filename, then tap the (ENTER) key to complete the rename command.
   Leave the My Computer window open.

Moving and Copying Files

Windows lets you move and copy files from one drive to another, and from one folder to another. There are several techniques you can use to move and copy files. This lesson will teach you three methods:

- **Copy and paste**—copies files into a new location.
- **Cut and paste**—moves files to a new location.
- **Drag-and-drop**—can either move or copy files to a new location.

QUICK REFERENCE: MOVING AND COPYING FILES WITH CUT, COPY, AND PASTE

Task	Procedure
Copy files with Copy and Paste.	■ Select the files to be copied.
	■ Click the Copy button on the toolbar, use the Edit→Copy command on the menu bar, or use (CTRL)+(C) from the keyboard.
	■ Navigate to the location in which the files are to be copied.
	■ Click the Paste button on the toolbar, use the Edit→Paste command on the menu bar, or use (CTRL)+(V) from the keyboard.
Move Files with Cut and Paste.	■ Select the files to be moved.
	■ Click the Cut button on the toolbar, use the Edit→Cut command on the menu bar, or use (CTRL)+(X) from the keyboard.
	■ Navigate to the location in which the files are to be moved.
	■ Click the Paste button on the toolbar, use the Edit→Paste command on the menu bar, or use (CTRL)+(V) from the keyboard.

Selecting Multiple Files for Move and Copy Commands

You can move and copy a single file or dozens of files with the same command. Before you give the Cut or Copy command, select the file(s) you wish to be affected by the command. To select a single file, you simply click on it. The two easiest methods of selecting multiple files are described in the Quick Reference table that follows. You can combine these two techniques as your needs dictate.

QUICK REFERENCE: HOW TO SELECT MULTIPLE FILES FOR COMMANDS

Technique	Procedure
(CTRL)+Click technique to select several files.	■ Click the first file you wish to select.
	■ Press and hold (CTRL) while you click on any other files you wish to select.
	■ Release the (CTRL) key when you have made all of your selections.
(SHIFT)+Click technique to select several files in a row.	■ Click the first file you wish to select.
	■ Press and hold (SHIFT) while you click last file in the group that you wish to select, then release (SHIFT).
Deselect a selected file.	■ Press and hold (CTRL) while you click on the file you wish to deselect.

See the Web page for this lesson to view a video on copying and moving files.

Hands-On 3.10 **Move and Copy Files**

Move a File with Cut and Paste

In this part of the exercise, you will use the Cut and Paste technique to move a single file into one of your new folders.

1. Make sure a My Computer window is displaying the 3½ Floppy (A:) drive. Look at the top-left corner of the My Computer window's title bar to confirm that you are at the right location.

2. Click to select the Map to Community Center file in the My Computer window.

3. Choose Edit→Cut from the menu bar.
   Notice that the icon for the file you selected is "dimmed." This indicates that the file has been cut and will be moved when you give the Paste command.

4. Double-click to open the Graphics folder.
   This navigates you to the empty Graphics folder.

5. Choose Edit→Paste from the menu bar.
   After the file has been moved, it will be displayed in the window.

NOTE!

The first level of a drive is also called the root.

6. Click the Up 🔼 or 📂 button on the toolbar to return to the 3½ Floppy (A:) drive level.
   Notice that the Map to Community Center file is no longer listed with the other files; it was moved to a different folder.

Copy Multiple Files

In this part of the exercise, you will select more than one file for the Copy and Paste commands.

7. Hold down the (CTRL) key as you click on the two Tutor Meeting document files, then release the (CTRL) key.
   Both files should now be selected.

8. Choose Edit→Copy from the menu bar.

9. Double-click to open the Documents folder.

10. Choose Edit→Paste from the menu bar.
    The files will appear in the window as they are copied.

11. Click the Up 🔼 or 📂 button on the toolbar to return to the 3½ Floppy (A:) drive level.
    Notice that the document files are still displayed in the window; they were copied rather than moved.

Moving and Copying Files with Drag-and-Drop

The Drag-and-Drop technique is an easy way to move or copy files or folders by dragging them to the desired location. The easiest way to use the Drag-and-Drop technique is to hold down the right (not the left) mouse button as you drag. This will give you a pop-up menu from which you select the Move or Copy command.

QUICK REFERENCE: MOVING AND COPYING FILES WITH DRAG AND DROP

Task	Procedure
Drag-and-Drop with the right-drag technique.	■ Select the files or folders to be moved or copied. ■ Point at one selected file or folder, press and hold the right mouse button, and drag the files or folders to the desired location. ■ Release the mouse button at the destination, then select Move Here, Copy Here, or Cancel from the pop-up menu.
Move files on the same disk drive with Drag-and-Drop.	■ Select the files or folders to be moved. ■ Point at one selected file or folder and drag with the left mouse button to a new location on the same disk drive.
Copy files to a different disk drive with Drag-and-Drop.	■ Select the files or folders to be copied. ■ Point at one selected file or folder and drag with the left mouse button to the new location on a different disk drive.

 ## Hands-On 3.11 Move Files with Drag and Drop

In this exercise, you will select two files with the (CTRL)+*Click technique.*

1. Click to select the Tutor Meeting file. Press (CTRL), click on the Tutor Meeting (September) document file, and release (CTRL).

2. Follow these steps to move the files with the Drag-and-Drop technique:
   The two files will disappear from the My Computer window as they are moved.

Ⓐ Point to one of the selected files, press and hold the right (not the left) mouse button, and drag the files onto the Graphics folder.

Ⓑ Release the right mouse button when the Graphics folder is selected (shaded), as shown here.

Ⓒ Choose Move Here from the pop-up menu.

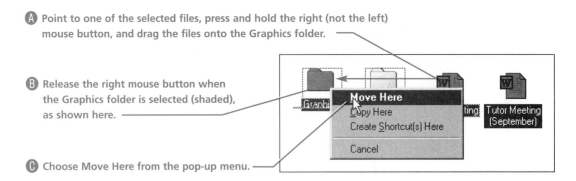

3. Double-click to open the Graphics folder.
   The two files you dragged and dropped should now be in the folder.

4. Click the Up ⬆ or 🗁 button on the toolbar to return to the 3½ Floppy (A:) drive level.

Deleting Files and Folders

You can delete files and folders by selecting them and clicking the Delete ⊠ button on the My Computer or Exploring window toolbar or tapping the (DELETE) key. When you delete a folder, any files inside that folder are deleted as well.

What Happens to Deleted Files?

Windows does not physically erase a deleted file from the hard drive. Instead, the file is placed in the Recycle Bin. The Recycle Bin holds the deleted files until you give a command to empty it, or it runs out of the space allotted to store deleted files. If you delete files from the hard drive, you can recover them by opening the Recycle Bin, selecting the files you wish to recover, then choosing File→Restore from the menu bar.

 WARNING! *Files and folders deleted from floppy disks are not sent to the Recycle Bin! They are permanently deleted when you issue the delete command.*

 Hands-On 3.12 Delete Files and a Folder

In this exercise, you will delete one of the files in the Documents folder. Then you will delete the Documents folder itself (erasing the other document file).

1. Double-click to open the Documents folder on your floppy disk.
   You still have a copy of these files in the Graphics folder, so it is safe to delete the ones in this folder.

2. Select one of the document files in the folder, then click the Delete ⊠ button on the toolbar or tap the (DELETE) key on the keyboard if the toolbar does not have a delete button.
   Depending on how Windows is configured, you may see a prompt asking if you really want to delete the file you selected. This is a safeguard to help prevent the accidental deletion of files. This confirmation feature can be switched on and off.

TIP!

Always make sure you know what's inside a folder before you delete it.

3. Click Yes if Windows asks you to confirm deleting the file.
   Windows will briefly display an animation of the files being deleted.

4. Click the Up 🔼 or 📁 button on the toolbar to return to the 3½ Floppy (A:) drive level.

5. Select the Documents folder, then click the Delete ⊠ button on the toolbar (or click Delete This Folder on the left side of the window if you are running Windows XP). Click Yes if Windows asks you to confirm deleting the folder and any of the files in it.

Checking Space on a Drive

As you create and save files to your floppy disk, the disk may eventually run out of space. Thus, you may want to check the space available on the floppy disk from time to time. You can use the Properties command to display a pie chart of the available space on a drive. Windows 2000 can also display a pie chart as part of a My Computer or Exploring window, as can all other versions of Windows if they are configured to do so.

QUICK REFERENCE: CHECKING THE AVAILABLE SPACE ON A DISK DRIVE

Task	Procedure
View a pie chart of how much space is available on a disk drive.	■ Open a My Computer or Exploring window.
	■ Right-click on the desired drive, then choose Properties from the pop-up menu.

 Hands-On 3.13 Check the Properties of Your Floppy Disk

In this exercise, you will find out how much space is available on your floppy disk using the Properties option.

1. Click the Up [image] or [image] button on the toolbar to return to the My Computer level in the computer system.

2. Follow these steps to view the properties of the floppy disk:

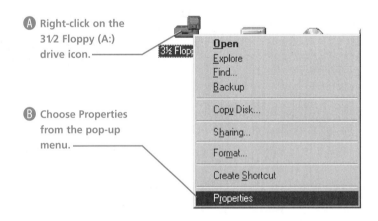

A Right-click on the 3 1/2 Floppy (A:) drive icon.

B Choose Properties from the pop-up menu.

A Properties window for the floppy drive will appear. The pie chart and numbers indicate how much space is available on the floppy disk.

3. Close ☒ the Properties window.

4. Click (don't double-click) on the 3½ Floppy (A:) drive.
Depending on how your version of Windows is configured, you may see a similar pie chart on the left side of the My Computer window.

5. Close ☒ the My Computer window.

The Exploring View

Windows gives you two ways of searching through files on the computer: the My Computer window and the Exploring Window. The My Computer window displays these items in a single panel. The Exploring window splits the display into two panels. Below is an example of an Exploring window.

This panel displays the structure of the computer's drives and folders.

This panel displays the contents of any drive or folder that you select for viewing. What you see in this panel is exactly the same as what you would see in a My Computer window.

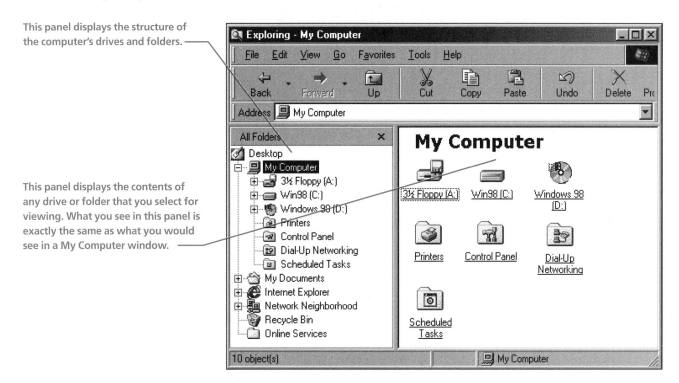

Why Two Views?

Microsoft researched the way people interact with computers. They found that most beginners are more comfortable with the single-panel view of the My Computer window. It is a simpler, more intuitive view of the computer system. Experienced users tend to prefer the flexibility of the Exploring window. They find it easier to navigate quickly in the computer with the Exploring view. Thus, providing both views satisfies the needs of beginners and experienced users.

You have used the My Computer window for most of the exercises in this lesson. Now you will have an opportunity to try the Exploring window. After you have tried both methods, you can decide which view works best for your file management activities. You may find that you prefer the My Computer view for the first year or two that you work with Windows. That's fine. You can perform the same tasks in either view.

See the Web page for this lesson to view a video on using the Exploring view.

QUICK REFERENCE: OPENING AN EXPLORING WINDOW

Task	Procedure
Open an Exploring Window.	You can use any of the following methods:

- Hold down the Windows (⊞) key on the keyboard and tap the (E) key.

- Right-click on the My Computer icon on the Desktop, then choose Explore from the pop-up menu.

- Right-click on the Start button, then choose Explore from the pop-up menu.

- Use the Start button menu command for your version of Windows:
  - Windows NT/2000/ME/XP—Choose Start→Programs→ Accessories→Windows Explorer.
  - Windows 98—Choose Start→Programs→Windows Explorer.

Hands-On 3.14 Launch an Exploring Window

In this exercise, you will launch an Exploring window and view your exercise diskette. Then, you will briefly view folders on the computer's hard drive.

1. Hold down the Windows (⊞) key on the keyboard, then tap the (E) key and release the Windows key.

   Note: If your keyboard does not have a windows key, use the Start button method (at the bottom of the Quick Reference table above) for your version of Windows.

   The Exploring window will appear.

2. If the Exploring window is not maximized, click the Maximize ▣ button. Choose View→Large Icons (or Icons) from the menu bar.

3. Follow these steps to navigate the folders on the 3½ Floppy (A:) drive in the Exploring window:

   Ⓐ Click the 3½ Floppy (A:) icon in the left panel to display the contents of the floppy drive in the right panel of the Exploring window.

   Ⓑ If necessary, click the + to expand the display of the folder inside the 3½ Floppy (A:) drive.

   Ⓒ Click the Graphics folder in the left panel.

   Ⓓ The files inside the Graphics folder are displayed in the right panel.

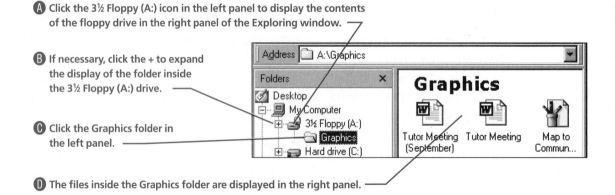

   The Exploring window makes navigating directly to folders on a floppy disk or hard drive easy to do. However, many beginners do not find it easy to look back and forth from the left panel to the right panel.

Move Files with Drag-and-Drop

4. Choose View→List from the menu bar.

5. Click on the first file in the list, and press (SHIFT), then click on the last file in the list.
The (SHIFT)+Click selection technique selects all of the files between your first and last click.

6. Click on one of the files (do not hold down the (SHIFT) key).
Now only the file you clicked is selected. To select more than one file, you must always hold down the (SHIFT) or (CTRL) key as you click additional files.

7. Choose Edit→Select All from the menu bar.
This command selects all of the files displayed in the right panel. This command is faster than the (CTRL)+Click or (SHIFT)+Click methods when you want to select all of the files in a folder.

8. Choose View→Large Icons (or Icons) from the menu bar.

9. Follow these steps to move the files back to the top level (root) of the floppy drive with the Drag-and-Drop technique:

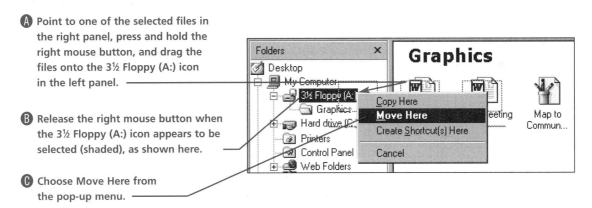

Ⓐ Point to one of the selected files in the right panel, press and hold the right mouse button, and drag the files onto the 3½ Floppy (A:) icon in the left panel.

Ⓑ Release the right mouse button when the 3½ Floppy (A:) icon appears to be selected (shaded), as shown here.

Ⓒ Choose Move Here from the pop-up menu.

When the Move command is completed, the Graphics folder will be empty.

10. Follow these steps to delete the empty Graphics folder:

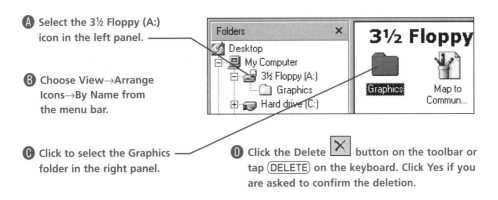

Ⓐ Select the 3½ Floppy (A:) icon in the left panel.

Ⓑ Choose View→Arrange Icons→By Name from the menu bar.

Ⓒ Click to select the Graphics folder in the right panel.

Ⓓ Click the Delete ✕ button on the toolbar or tap (DELETE) on the keyboard. Click Yes if you are asked to confirm the deletion.

(Continued on the next page)

Explore the Hard Drive

Compared to your floppy disk, a typical hard drive stores many thousands more files in a much more complex folder structure. Now you will browse a few of the folders on a hard drive.

11. Follow these steps to browse folders on the hard drive:

Ⓐ Click the plus sign (+) next to the Hard drive (C:) to expand the view of folders on this drive. The C: drive may not be named the same as the illustration.

Ⓑ Click the plus sign (+) next to the Program Files folder to expand the view of other folders inside this folder. This folder holds most of the application programs installed on the computer. There may be dozens of folders here.

Ⓒ Select the Accessories folder. Depending on the version of Windows you are running and what has been installed, there may only be one or two items in this folder. The contents of the Accessories folder is now displayed in the right panel.

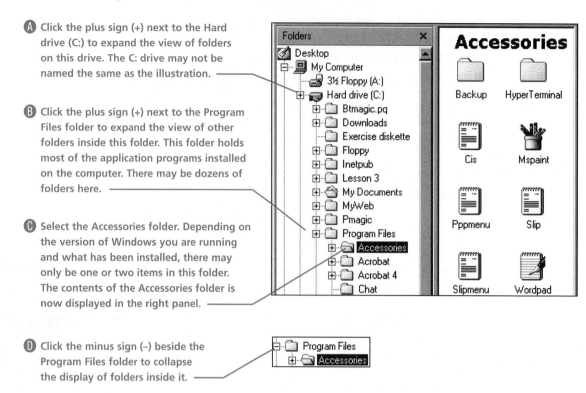

Ⓓ Click the minus sign (–) beside the Program Files folder to collapse the display of folders inside it.

12. Close ✖ the Exploring window.

Concepts Review

True/False Questions

1. A Contents (or Home in Windows ME and XP) search of online Help lets you locate Help topics by typing keywords.   TRUE   FALSE

2. A My Computer window lets you view the files and folders on the computer.   TRUE   FALSE

3. Windows organizes drives and folders in a hierarchy.   TRUE   FALSE

4. You can use the (CTRL) key to randomly select a group of files.   TRUE   FALSE

5. Folders can have subfolders within them.   TRUE   FALSE

6. You can use the Cut and Paste commands to move files.   TRUE   FALSE

7. Files are sent to the Recycle Bin when they are deleted from floppy disks.   TRUE   FALSE

8. The Properties command displays how much space is left on a floppy disk.   TRUE   FALSE

9. An Exploring window gives you a two-panel view of files and folder.   TRUE   FALSE

10. A quick way to open a file is to double-click on it in a My Computer windows.   TRUE   FALSE

Multiple-Choice Questions

1. Which of the following methods would you use to view files and folders on the computer:
   a. Open a My Computer Window
   b. Open an Exploring Window
   c. Both A and B
   d. None of the Above

2. Which of the following views displays columns with the filename, size, type, and modified date?
   a. Large Icons
   b. Small Icons
   c. List
   d. Details
   e. Thumbnails

3. Which command is used to create a new folder?
   a. File→Folder→Create
   b. File→New→Folder
   c. Click the 🗀 or 🗋 button
   d. All of the above

4. If one filename is already selected in a My Computer or Exploring window, which key could be used to select several more files by clicking just once?
   a. (SHIFT)
   b. (ALT)
   c. (CTRL)
   d. None of the above

Skill Builders

Skill Builder 3.1 **Work with Online Help**

In this exercise, you will practice looking up various topics in Windows' online Help.

1. Click the ![Start] button and choose Help from the Start menu. Maximize ▢ the Help Window.

2. Choose the Index search method in the Help window.

3. Start typing the search keywords **recycle bin**. You will notice that the phrase Recycle Bin appears after you type the letters recy.
   You usually only need to type the first few characters of the desired search phrase.

4. Double-click to open the topic according to the operating system you are running:

   ■ **Windows 98:** Recycle Bin

   ■ **Windows NT:** Recycle Bin, then choose To Empty The Recycle Bin

   ■ **Windows 2000:** emptying

   ■ **Windows ME:** Recycle Bin, then choose To empty the Recycle Bin

   ■ **Windows XP:** emptying

5. Read the topic. If you are running Windows 95 or NT, click the Help Topics button near the top-left corner of the window to return to the Index search window.

6. Use the Index search method to get Help on the following topics.

Windows Version	Search Keyword(s)	Help Topics to Open
Windows NT	My Computer	opening files or folders
	Windows Explorer	changing the way items are displayed
	Copying	files or folders→copying a file or folder
	drag-and-drop	using drag and drop instead of menus
Windows 98	My Computer	opening files→to open a file or folder
	Windows Explorer	checking disk space
	copying files, folders	overview
	dragging files, folders	to move a file or folder
Windows 2000	My Computer	opening files or folders
	Windows Explorer	copying files or folders
	copying files	overview→copy or move a file or folder
	dragging files	overview→move files by dragging
Windows ME	my computer	to open a file or folder
	windows explorer	sorting items in
	copying files	overview
	selecting	selecting, files, folders
Windows XP	my computer	overview
	windows explorer	copy files and folders by dragging
	copying files	files and folders overview
	selecting	selecting multiple files and folders...

These Help topics will give you tips and alternatives to the methods you have already learned.

7. Click the Contents tab (or Home if you are running Windows ME or XP).

8. Choose a topic according to the operating system you are running:

   ■ **Windows NT:** How to: Working with files and folders

   ■ **Windows 98:** Exploring your computer: Files and folders: Managing Files

   ■ **Windows 2000:** Files and folders

   ■ **Windows ME**: Programs, Files, & Folders: Managing files & folders

   ■ **Windows XP**: Windows basics: Core Windows tasks: working with files and folders

9. Locate five different Help Sub-topics for the topic listed above for your operating system. Take the time to open the Help topics and read them.

10. Experiment with Help until you are confident that you can find topics when the need arises, using the most efficient search method.

11. Close the Help window ☒.

Skill Builder 3.2 **Create a Folder**

In this exercise, you will create a new folder.

1. Open a My Computer window, and double-click the 3½ Floppy (A:) drive to display the files on your exercise diskette. If necessary, maximize the window.

2. Double-click the Map to Community Center file.
   The Paint program, or another program assigned to open Paint files will launch, and your map will be displayed in the program window.

   ■ **Windows XP Only**: This version of Windows may open the map in a viewer. Click the Edit File button as shown at the right to open the Paint file in the Paint program.

3. Close ☒ the Paint (or other program) window. Click No if you are asked to save the file.

4. Choose the Details view, then click on the Modified heading to sort the files by date.

5. Use File→New→Folder to create a folder on your exercise diskette named **Backup**. If the folder name is not selected when you create it, right-click on the folder icon, then use the Rename command to change the name.

Skill Builder 3.3a **Copy Files in Windows 98 and NT 4.0**

TIP!

Use the (CTRL)
or (SHIFT) *key to*
select multiple
files.

Note: In this exercise, you will copy files to the new Backup folder, then delete them.

Skip this exercise and perform Skill Builder 3.3b if you are not running Windows 98 or NT 4.0.

1. A My Computer window should be open, displaying the contents of the 3½ Floppy (A:) drive with the Details view.

2. Click the Size column heading to sort the list of files by size, then select the two smallest files on your diskette.

3. Click the copy [icon] button on the My Computer toolbar.

4. Double-click the Backup folder.

5. Click the Paste [icon] button on the My Computer toolbar.
   After the Copy operation is completed, the two files you selected should appear in the folder.

6. Click the Up [icon] button on the My Computer toolbar.
   The two files that you copied should still be visible at the top level (root) of your exercise diskette. For the moment, these files exist in two locations on the floppy disk.

7. Select the Backup folder, then delete the folder.

8. Close [icon] the My Computer window.

Skill Builder 3.3b **Copy Files in Windows 2000, ME, and XP**

In this exercise, you will copy files to the new Backup folder, then delete them.

 Windows 2000, ME, and XP use two new toolbar buttons that help you move and copy files from one folder to another. The Move to and Copy to buttons allow you to navigate to the destination for the move or copy command in a special dialog box. This Skill Builder exercise gives you the opportunity to try this new method.

TIP!

Use the (CTRL)
or (SHIFT) *key to*
select multiple
files.

1. A My Computer window should be open, displaying the contents of the 3½ Floppy (A:) drive with the Details view.

2. Click the Size column heading to sort the list of files by size, then select the two smallest files on your diskette.

3. **Windows 2000 and ME:** Click the Copy To [icon] button on the toolbar.

   Windows XP: Click the Copy the Selected Items task in the File and Folder Tasks section of the window, as shown below.

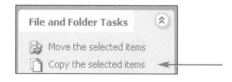

4. Follow these steps to select the destination of the Copy command:

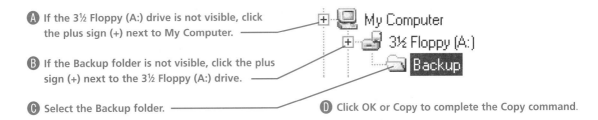

A If the 3½ Floppy (A:) drive is not visible, click the plus sign (+) next to My Computer.

B If the Backup folder is not visible, click the plus sign (+) next to the 3½ Floppy (A:) drive.

C Select the Backup folder.

D Click OK or Copy to complete the Copy command.

5. Double-click to open the Backup folder and verify that the files were copied.
   The two files you selected should appear in the folder.

6. Click the Up 🔼 or 🗁 button on the My Computer toolbar.

7. Select the Backup folder, then delete the folder.

8. Close ☒ the My Computer window.

Skill Builder 3.4 Check the Hard Drive Properties

In this exercise, you will determine the amount of space left on your hard drive and floppy disk.

1. In a My Computer window, right-click on the (C:) drive icon, then choose Properties from the pop-up menu.

2. Write down how much free space there is left on the hard drive: _____
   Many megabytes, or even gigabytes, of space will probably be available on the hard drive.

Look at the number on the right. ─────

3. Click Cancel to close the Properties window.

4. Make sure your exercise diskette is in the floppy drive.

5. Check the properties of your exercise diskette.

6. Write down how much free space is left on your exercise diskette: _____
   The amount of space left your diskette will be quite small compared to the hard drive.

7. Click Cancel to close the Properties window.

8. Close the ☒ My Computer window.

 **Assessments**

Assessment 3.1 **Search Online Help**

1. Start the WordPad program.

2. Type your name at the top of the WordPad document, tap (ENTER) twice, type **Shutting Down the Computer,** then tap (ENTER).

3. Start Windows online Help and look up the following topic: shutting down the computer. (Do not try to look up the topic in WordPad's online Help.)

   ■ **Windows XP only:** Search for a topic on Turning Off the computer.

4. Arrange the Help and WordPad windows one above the other or side-by-side so that the Help window is visible as you type in WordPad. Remember that you cannot change the size of a maximized window.

5. In WordPad, type the first line of instructions for the Help topic, then tap the (ENTER) key twice.

6. Type **Creating a Folder**, then tap (ENTER).

7. Look up the following topic in Windows online Help: creating a folder or creating new folders.

8. In WordPad, type the first three steps of the instructions for the Help topic, then tap the (ENTER) key twice.

9. Save the WordPad document to your exercise diskette as **Online Help**.

10. Print the document and turn it in to your instructor for grading.

11. Close ☒ the WordPad and Help windows.

Assessment 3.2 **Create a Folder and Copy Files**

1. Open a My Computer or Exploring window.

2. Create a folder on your exercise diskette named **Lesson 3**.

3. Copy the Tutor Meeting and the Tutor Meeting (September) files to the new folder.

4. Close ☒ the My Computer or Exploring window.

Assessment 3.3 Navigate in an Exploring Window

1. Open an Exploring (not a My Computer) window.

2. Display your exercise diskette in the Exploring window.

3. Display the contents of the Lesson 3 folder in the right panel of the Exploring window.

4. Have your instructor or a lab assistant initial that you have performed this assessment successfully.   _____

Glossary of Terms

Term	Description	Example
24-bit color	Level of color resolution that allows the display of millions of colors on the monitor	See *Computer Video* (page 14)
AGP port	Short for **A**ccelerated **G**raphics **P**ort; a special slot designed for the display of high-speed 3-D graphics	
Anti-virus program	Software designed to stop computer viruses from infecting files on the computer	Norton Antivirus
Application program	Software designed to help you get work done	Microsoft Word, Lotus 1-2-3
ASCII	Standard code for representing alphabetic, numeric, and symbolic characters on the computer	See *Units of Measure* (page 6)
Benchmark	Program that tests the performance of a computer system	Winbench, Winstone
Bit	Single on-off switch in a computer circuit	0, 1.
Byte	Single character of data; it is composed of 8 bits in a specific order	A, B, C, etc
Cable modem	Device designed to send and receive digital data over television cable system wiring	
Cache	Form of high-speed RAM designed to temporarily store the most recently processed software code	512K L2 cache
Cathode ray tube (CRT)	Technology used by large, television-style monitors; CRT monitors are gradually being replaced by thinner, more efficient LCD panels	
Data bus	Channel by which data is transmitted from expansion cards and RAM to the microprocessor	PCI, ISA, AGP
Digital camera	Still camera that stores images as computer files rather than on film; most connect to a computer via a USB cable	Nikon Coolpix 5000
Digital video camera	Video camera that records images to digital tape or disk; specially designed to transfer video directly to a computer's hard drive via a firewire port	Sony Handycam
Dots per inch (DPI)	Measure of the sharpness of a printer's output; the higher the dots per inch, the sharper the print will appear on the page	600 DPI (laser printer)
Ergonomics	Science of creating work environments and furnishings well-tuned to the shape and function of the human body	Natural (split) keyboards
Expansion card	Electronic component that adds new capabilities to the computer	Internal modem, video capture
File	Group of computer data with a common purpose	A letter you have typed, a program
Firewire port	Also called the IEEE 1394 port; popular for connecting digital video cameras and other high-speed peripherals	A connector on a digital video camera
Gigabyte	Approximately one billion bytes of data	About 3,000 books

Term	Description	Example
Gigahertz (GHz)	One billion pulses of electricity in an electrical circuit in a single second; the speed of most microprocessors sold today is measured in gigahertz	3.0 GHz
Hardware	Physical components of a computer system	Disk drive, monitor, microprocessor
Hertz (Hz)	Single pulse of electricity in an electrical circuit	See *Refresh Rate* on page 15
IDE	Type of controller for disk drives	IDE hard drive
IEEE 1394	See Firewire port	
Kilobyte (KB)	Approximately one thousand bytes of data	One single-spaced page of text
Kilohertz (kHz)	One thousand electrical pulses per second; the speed of older microprocessors is measured in kilohertz	800-kHz Pentium III microprocessor
LCD Panel	Monitor that uses liquid crystal display technology to create the screen image rather than a cathode ray tube (CRT) as in earlier monitors	
Macro virus	Computer virus transmitted in infected word processor documents and spreadsheet files	Form virus
Megabyte (MB)	Approximately one million bytes of data	3 average-length novels
Megahertz (MHz)	One million pulses of electricity in an electrical circuit in a single second	266MHz (microprocessor clock speed rating)
Microprocessor	One single silicon chip containing the complete circuitry of a computer	Intel Pentium II, AMD K6, Intel Celleron
Modem	Device that lets a computer communicate digital data to other computers over analog telephone lines	28.8K modem
Monitor	The computer screen	15" monitor
MP3	Acronym for **M**oving **P**icture Experts Group Layer-**3** Audio; first popular format for highly compressed music files	A music file
Parallel port (also called LPT1)	Connection at the back of the system unit; printers are commonly connected to the parallel port	See *Ports* (page 20)
Peripherals	Hardware components outside the system unit	Monitor, keyboard
Pixel	A single dot of light on a computer monitor	See illustration on page 14
Port	A place at the back of the computer to plug in a cable	Parallel port, serial port
RAM	Short for **r**andom **a**ccess **m**emory; computer chip designed to temporarily store data to be processed	32MB RAM
Refresh rate	How often the computer's display is redrawn each second; a refresh rate of 70 Hertz or more gives a flicker-free display that is easy on the eyes	70Hz

Term	Description	Example
Resolution	Measure of the sharpness of a computer monitor display or a printout	640x480 (monitor) 300 DPI (printer)
Scanner	Device that turns photographs and other images into computer files	HP Scanjet 5p
SCSI port	Pronounced "scuzzy"; short for Small Computer Systems Interface; commonly used to connect disk drives and scanners to the computer	
Serial port (also called COM1 and COM2)	Most computers have two serial connections at the back of the system unit; modems and mice are commonly connected to serial ports	
Software	Logical component of a computer system; composed of digital code stored in the form of files; some software exists as programs to help you get work done; also stores work	Windows 98, Internet Explorer, a document file
System unit	Main box that contains the primary components of the computer	See *Computer Systems* (page 4)
Terabyte (TB)	Approximately one trillion bytes of data	About 30,000 books.
USB port	Short for Universal Serial Bus port; a single USB port can connect several devices simultaneously, including keyboards, scanners, modems, cameras, and more; USB 2.0 standard transfers data about 40 times faster than the original USB 1.0 port	See page 21
VGA, SVGA	Short for Video Graphics Array; VGA compatible monitors display the computer screen in a variety of color and resolution settings	SVGA monitor
Virus	Program that invisibly "infects" files and disrupts operation of a computer in some way	Michelangelo, Good News
WMA	Acronym for Windows Media Audio; a recent audio format for compressing music files with better performance than available from the MP3 format	A music file

Index